Step by Step to Comprehensive School Health

The Program Planning Guide

William M. Kane, PhD, CHES

E T R   A S S O C I A T E S
Santa Cruz, California
1993

ETR Associates (Education, Training and Research) is a nonprofit organization committed to fostering the health, well-being and cultural diversity of individuals, families, schools and communities. The publishing program of ETR Associates provides books and materials that empower young people and adults with the skills to make positive health choices. We invite health professionals to learn more about our high-quality publishing, training and research programs by contacting us at P.O. Box 1830, Santa Cruz, CA 95061-1830.

About the Author

William M. Kane, PhD, CHES, is associate professor of health education at the University of New Mexico in Albuquerque. He is a former public school teacher and coordinator of health education and an author of health education textbooks. He has served as executive director of two national health organizations, the Association for the Advancement of Health Education and the American College of Preventive Medicine, and has been active in the establishment of many national health education initiatives.

Published by ETR Associates, P.O. Box 1830, Santa Cruz, California 95061-1830

Printed in the United States of America

10 9 8 7 6 5 4 3

Cover design by Detta Penna
Text design by Ann Smiley

Title No. 562

Kane, William, 1947–
    Step by step to comprehensive school health : the program planning guide / William M. Kane.
      p. cm.
    Includes bibliographical references (p. 137).
    1. Health education (Elementary)—United States. 2. Health education (Secondary)—United States. 3. Health education—United States—Curricula. 4. Community and school—United States. I. Title.
LB1588.U6K36   1993
613'.017'073—dc20   92-39987

Contents

Tables, Figures and Worksheets

Preface

This guide was developed for use by parents, elected school officials, administrators, community leaders and teachers who believe that the schools can provide opportunities for all students to develop healthy behaviors that will enable them to reach their fullest potential. To create these healthy schools, the following ingredients are necessary:

- an understanding of the health risks faced by youth

- commitment and cooperation between the community, home and school to provide a safe environment.

- learning experiences that enable young people to acquire the health knowledge and skills essential to adoption of healthy behaviors

- a safe and supportive learning environment that provides opportunities for students and staff to practice healthy behaviors

- support and reinforcement, which increases the possibility that healthy behaviors will become lifelong health habits

The step-by-step approach presented here enables school administrators to organize the school in a way that promotes health and to structure healthy learning experiences for students. The theoretical and scientific information important to understanding students' needs is outlined, and approaches that have proven successful in other schools are described in terms that allow for easy implementation. Guidelines, figures and worksheets to assist school leaders with the development of a comprehensive school health program are provided.

Healthy People 2000: National Health Promotion and Disease Prevention Objectives, the U.S. Public Health Service plan for improving the health of all Americans by the year 2000, simply states the obvious: "To arrive at the established goals...[healthy children], we must chart a common course that depends upon commitment and action from every level of our society" (U.S. Department of Health and Human Services, 1990).

Healthy People 2000 goes on to recommend that schools have a special role in enhancing and maintaining the health of their communities' children. It advocates a partnership between parents, schools and other community groups to create health promotion programs and enhance health education curricula.

The need for a collaborative venture between parents, families, communities and schools aimed at helping children grow up healthy is clear. *Step by Step to Comprehensive School Health* helps school leaders assess their school's current readiness for promoting the health of students, establish goals, and develop a planning and implementation process. This process should build on the aspirations and commitment of parents, school leaders and communities to ensure that all children have the opportunity to achieve optimal health and reach

their maximal potential.

Children are the future of the world. This book will enable leaders to develop plans that help schools and communities treat children as our world's most valuable resource.

J. Michael McGinnis, MD, director of the U.S. Office of Disease Prevention and Health Promotion, has identified the following objective as the "sentinel objective in *Healthy People 2000* for school health" (McGinnis and DeGraw, 1991):

By the year 2000: Increase to at least 75 percent the proportion of the nation's elementary and secondary schools that provide planned and sequential kindergarten through 12th grade quality school health education (Objective #8.4).

School leaders who accept the challenge of developing comprehensive school-based programs that promote student health will be utilizing the most systematic and efficient means available to improve the health of youth, improve learning opportunities and help our youth avoid future health risks. *Step by Step to Comprehensive School Health* provides school leaders with a framework and the tools for making this goal a reality.

Acknowledgments

I would like to acknowledge the leadership that ETR Associates has provided for the development of school health programs. The organization, through its leadership in publications, inservice education and research, has translated the theory and science of health promotion into practical materials for use in schools throughout America.

Specifically, I would like to thank Kathleen Middleton and ETR Associates' publishing staff for their technical assistance and patience with me during the development of this publication.

Special thanks also goes to the following professionals for their critical and helpful reviews:

David A. Birch, PhD, CHES
Director, Health Outreach Programs
Dept. of Health Education
The Pennsylvania State University

Joyce V. Fetro, PhD, CHES
Health Education Specialist
San Francisco Unified School District

Sherman K. Sowby, PhD, CHES
Professor of Health Science
California State University, Fresno

1

Why Comprehensive School Health?

Children are the future of America, the world and civilization. Our aspirations, our hopes and our dreams are closely linked to our children's ability to learn and to develop skills and to use their knowledge and skills for the betterment of humankind. The quality of life we ultimately achieve is determined in large part by the health decisions we make, the subsequent behaviors we adopt, and the public policies that promote and support the establishment of healthy behaviors.

A healthy child is capable of growing and learning; of producing new knowledge and ideas; of sharing, interacting and living peacefully with others in a complex and changing society. Fostering healthy children is the shared responsibility of families, communities and schools.

Health behaviors, the most important predictors of current and future health status, are influenced by a variety of factors. Factors that lead to and support

children's establishment of healthy behaviors include:

- awareness and knowledge of health issues
- the skills necessary to practice healthy behaviors
- opportunities to practice healthy behaviors
- support and reinforcement for the practice of healthy behaviors

When young people receive reinforcement for the practice of a healthy behavior, they feel good about the healthy behavior. Reinforcement and the subsequent good feeling increase the likelihood that an individual will continue to practice a behavior and thereby establish a positive health habit. The good feeling and the experience of success motivate young people to place a high value on the behavior (e.g., being a nonsmoker is good).

The perception that a particular healthy behavior is worthwhile often results in young people becoming advocates, encouraging others to adopt the healthy behavior. When these young advocates exert pressure on peers to adopt healthy behaviors, a healthy social norm is established (e.g., tobacco use is unacceptable in this school).

Because health behaviors are learned, they can be shaped and changed. Partner-

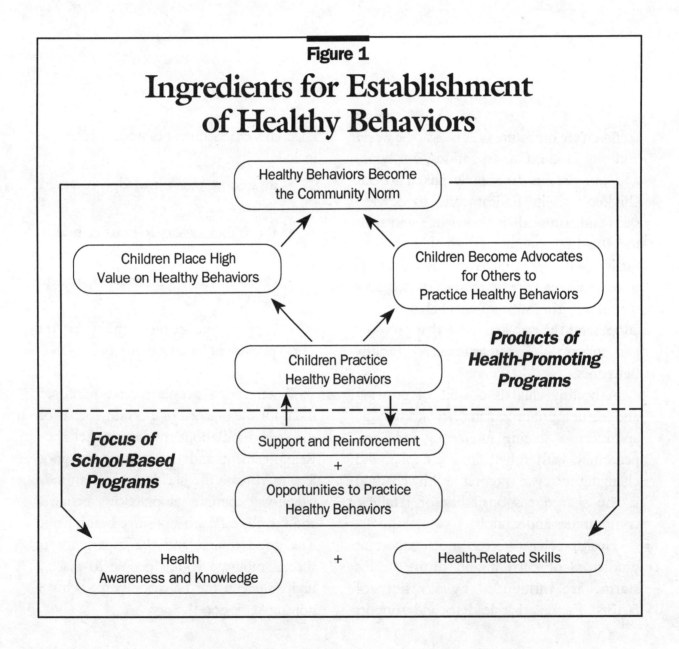

Figure 1

Ingredients for Establishment of Healthy Behaviors

ships between family members, community leaders, teachers and school leaders are a vital key to the initial development and maintenance of children's healthy behaviors and can also play a role in the modification of unhealthy behaviors. Schools, perhaps more than any other single agency in our society, have the opportunity to influence factors that shape the future health and productivity of Americans.

The Role of the School

In 1990 the National Commission on the Role of the School and Community in Improving Adolescent Health issued the following statement, urging schools to play a stronger role in improving adolescent health:

Schools should recognize that they can only accomplish their education mission if they attend to students' emotional, social and physical needs. Schools should become far more personal institutions and more positive learning environments that engage adolescents' interest and motivate them to achieve their potential. They should offer students a new type of health education that provides honest, relevant information and teaches skills and strategies to make wise decisions and develop positive values. They should assure schools are smoke free, drug free and violence free, and promote the emotional and physical wellness of students and staff. They should make arrangements for students to receive needed services, increasing their own service capacity and establishing collaborative relationships with external agencies (p. 233).

The commission called upon this nation to recognize that adolescents will not achieve their potential if they have social, emotional or physical health problems that interfere with their learning. The commission concluded the executive summary by stating, "...the future is bleak if we do not invest more in our nation's greatest resource—our young people."

Although the commission specifically addressed the needs of adolescents, the recommendations are pertinent to children and youth of all ages. A series of recommendations for improving the health of adolescents was issued by the commission. Those recommendations pertinent to education follow.

Educators should:

• Recognize that education and health are inextricably intertwined and that achieving their education mission will require attending to the health needs of the students.

• Recognize the necessity of working with not only adolescents, but their families, whatever the composition of the families might be.

• Be advocates or ensure that there are advocates for troubled adolescents.

Teachers, administrators and other school personnel should:

• Make health a key consideration in school improvement plans—both with regard to making schools "more personal" and creating other ways to make schools better health-promoting environments.

• Provide a new kind of health education at the earliest appropriate age—an education that ensures that all students have the knowledge and skills to lead healthy lives and avoid health-risking behaviors.

• Promote the concept of collaboration within the school and welcome other health professionals and service delivery organizations to the school as full partners in working with adolescents.

School officials should:

• Afford school personnel sufficient time to work with troubled adolescents on a one-on-one basis.

• Permit sharing of information with collaborating agencies on a need-to-know basis that maintains confidentiality.

• Allow schools to serve as locations for adolescent health care if the local community determines that school sites are the most effective location for providing collaborative services.

• Make school sites available as sites for recreation, services and other community activities outside school hours.

• Provide all students opportunities to engage in community service.

The commission also recognized that improving the health of adolescents would require contributions and sacrifices from all sectors of society. In addition to recommendations for educational leaders, they delineated the roles of adolescents, families and individuals; federal and state governments; local communities including the health community, churches and youth-serving organizations; businesses; and the media, entertainment and advertising industries. School leaders need to base their health education programs on this broad perspective of healthy children and youth and this shared family, community and school responsibility.

A report of the Carnegie Corporation Task Force on Education of Young Adolescents called on schools to "...capitalize on the young person's natural curiosity about bodily changes and the transition to adulthood by integrating education for health with life sciences education" (Carnegie Council on Adolescent Development, 1989). The report viewed adolescents' understanding of biology and behavior as crucial to developing the ability to make healthy choices related to substance use, diet, exercise, sexuality and other aspects of health.

Indeed, schools do have special opportunities to prepare children and youth to establish health-promoting behaviors:

- Schools, guided by boards of education, are extensions of the family and community and provide mechanisms for helping communities and families achieve their aspirations.

- School leaders and teachers are parents and community members who share aspirations for the future of children and the world.

- Children spend about six hours each school day in classroom and school activities centered around learning.

- Teachers have specific knowledge regarding physical and social development of children, as well as the opportunity to compare the developmental level of children of similar age, gender and social background.

- Teachers and school personnel are professionally prepared in techniques for assessing children's needs, organizing learning opportunities, guiding students' learning and development, assessing progress and interacting with other school personnel to support development of children.

- The school is organized around classroom instruction, an important tool in helping children acquire skills and health knowledge for daily living.

- Teachers have training in shaping and reinforcing desired behaviors.

- Classroom teachers who model healthy behavior can have an important impact in shaping the healthy behavior of students.

- Kids teaching kids, or peer learning, is a powerful educational tool. It provides an excellent opportunity to introduce, model and reinforce social skills and health behaviors.

- The environmental factors conducive to protecting, supporting and reinforcing healthy behaviors are within direct control of school leaders.

The 1990 report of the National Health/Education Consortium (Amidei, 1990), involving more than forty health, medical and education organizations, proclaimed that "since risky behaviors are usually well established by high school age, linking health with education must begin very early in life." The report pointed out that key risk factors of pregnancy can be changed with education. It also noted that significant long-lasting health gains for young children could be achieved by combining health with education.

Healthy People 2000: National Health Promotion and Disease Prevention Objectives set forth a national strategy for significantly improving the health of the nation through the 1990s. It identifies school health programs as a key to attaining the target objectives. In developing or reviewing school health programs, school leaders need to consider the language used in *Healthy People 2000* to describe school health programs:

Health education in the school set-ting is especially important for helping children and youth develop the increas-ingly complex knowledge and skills they will need to avoid health risks and maintain good health throughout life. Quality school health education that is planned and sequential for students in kindergarten through twelfth grade, and taught by educators trained to teach the subject, has been shown to be effective in preventing risk behaviors.

Quality school health education addresses and integrates education, skills development, and motivation on a range of health problems and issues (e.g., nutrition; physical activity; injury control; use of tobacco, alcohol and other drugs; sexual behaviors that result in HIV infection, other sexually transmitted diseases and unintended pregnancies)

at developmentally appropriate ages. The content of health education is determined locally by parents, school boards and other members of the community (p. 251).

Other aspects of the school environment important to school health were identified in *Healthy People 2000*. The report urged school leaders to work with state and local health departments to provide a multi-dimensional program of school health. Such a program includes school health education; a healthy and safe environment; school-linked or school-based health services designed to prevent, detect and address health problems; physical education; healthy school food service selections; psychological assessment and counseling to promote child develop-ment and emotional health; schoolsite health promotion for faculty and staff; and integrated school and community health promotion efforts.

The Foundation of Effective School Health Programs

The sources of information to help school leaders develop effective school health programs lie in family and community values and aspirations for young people; the resources of communities, families and schools; and epidemiologic data. In addi-tion, educational and behavioral science theory and the results of evaluation research identify successful program features, learning and teaching strategies, and opportunities that support development of healthy youth. This information is the foundation upon which school leaders can develop effective school health programs.

Identifying Family and Community Values and Aspirations

A clear understanding of the values, aspirations and priorities of the families and communities in which students live provides a starting point for school leaders who want to develop and implement an effective school health program. This understanding enables school leaders to work with families and community members to develop a statement that articulates a shared vision for the health of children.

Developing a statement of shared vision that reflects family and community values is a critical first step in developing a comprehensive school health program. School leaders need to ask the following questions:

- What values are important for families and members of this community?
- How do these values affect school children's opportunities for good health?
- What are the community's and families' priorities for their children?
- What are the community and family values that support (or don't support) healthy development of youth?
- Are there other measures of quality of life important to the community?

Families and communities, regardless of their economic and social status, have high aspirations for their children. School and community leaders need to work with families to identify these aspirations and build programs that effectively integrate and

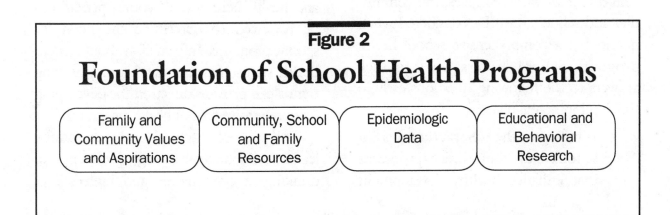

Figure 2

Foundation of School Health Programs

| Family and Community Values and Aspirations | Community, School and Family Resources | Epidemiologic Data | Educational and Behavioral Research |

nurture these hopes. Engaging families and youth in discussions regarding their hopes and dreams is the first step in identifying and building on these dreams.

There are many techniques available for identifying and assessing the community's values and aspirations for its children. For example:

- questionnaires to survey parents and students

- personal interviews with community leaders

- open town-hall meetings

- group discussions with parents and students

- open call-in telephone line

- drop-in centers in shopping malls or other public places

Assessing Community, School and Family Resources

The resources within families, the community and schools must be considered when developing a comprehensive school health program. School leaders need to seek answers to the following questions early in the developmental phase:

- What are the characteristics of school and community programs that enhance healthy development of youth?

- Who are the community representatives that need to be brought together to devise programs to support the healthy development of youth?

- What resources currently exist within the school, family and community to support the healthy development of youth?

- What underdeveloped or undeveloped resources exist within the school, family and community to support the healthy development of youth?

- What resources exist within the children themselves (e.g., does the school have a peer educator program)?

Using Epidemiologic Data for Program Planning

Epidemiologic data is another source of information essential to the establishment of school health programs. National, state and local data regarding the health status and health behaviors of young people can be reviewed to determine the need for specific programs. Information about current health status (baseline data) and emerging trends can provide direction for developing comprehensive school health programs.

For example, school and community leaders who discover a high prevalence of drinking among middle and high school students may use this information to develop a range of school-based programs. Programs aimed at preventing or delaying the onset of drinking behavior could be developed for elementary and middle schools, and student assistance programs aimed at early identification of and intervention in alcohol use could be developed at the middle and high school levels.

Health status and behavioral risk factor data related to youth can also be used to generate community awareness, interest and support for establishing effective comprehensive school health programs. Newspaper articles highlighting these issues can accompany the announcement of the school's intent to establish an initiative focusing on the health of children and youth.

Monitoring the health status and prevalence of behavioral risk factors in school-age youth can help schools establish target objectives and determine the effectiveness of comprehensive school health programs. Epidemiological data on health status and behavioral risk factors can also act as a baseline upon which to measure the longitudinal success of health intervention.

An example of this approach is the U.S. Department of Health and Human Services' "Health Promotion and Disease Prevention Objectives for the Year 2000," set forth in *Healthy People 2000*. More than one hundred target health objectives that can either be directly attained by schools or influenced in important ways by schools have

been identified in that document. Each target objective sets a goal for improvement in health for the year 2000. Baseline data (1988–1990) stating the current status are identified for each objective.

The following is an example of a drug-related student target objective identified in *Healthy People 2000*:

Objective #4.10

Increase the proportion of high school seniors who associate risk of physical or psychological harm with the heavy use of alcohol, regular use of marijuana and experimentation with cocaine, as follows:

Behavior	Baseline 1989	Target 2000
Heavy Use of Alcohol	44%	70%
Regular Use of Marijuana	75.5%	90%
Trying Cocaine Once or Twice	54.9%	80%

The 1989 baseline data enable schools to measure progress in their efforts to increase students' understanding of the dangers of alcohol and other drug use over time.

The data most useful to school leaders are reports from the local school or school district. When data specific to schools or the district are unavailable, school leaders will want to consider city, county or state data sets. Specific questions school leaders should ask include:

- What are the leading causes of mortality (deaths) among school-age children and youth in this community?

- What are the leading causes of morbidity (sickness and injury) among school-age children and youth in this community?

- What are the unhealthy or risky behaviors of our children and youth that will result in future morbidity and mortality?

- At what age do our children and youth develop these unhealthy or risky behaviors?

There are many sources of data regarding health status and health behavior of children and youth that can guide school efforts to establish relevant comprehensive school health programs. The sources of these data include federal, state and local government reports, and research conducted by private and voluntary organizations interested in the health of children.

State, County and Local Department of Health Vital Records and Health Statistics Annual Reports

These reports, obtainable from state health departments, provide an overview of selected vital and health statistics. To portray pat-

terns of temporal change, data from earlier years is included in the reports. Data of interest to school leaders in these reports include causes of death by age-grouping, communicable disease patterns (including sexually transmitted disease and HIV infection), births to teenage women and birth-related health problems among young mothers resulting from unhealthy practices and insufficient prenatal care. These data are most often displayed on a county by county basis. Large cities often have their own health statistics reports.

Federal Government Surveys

Monitoring the Youth Survey: A Study of the Lifestyles and Values of Youth is an annual survey established in 1975 by the National Institute of Drug Abuse. It surveys a nationally representative sample of more than 16,000 high school seniors and reports prevalence and trends of substance use and factors that may explain changes in substance use patterns.

The U.S. Office of Disease Prevention and Health Promotion's *National Adolescent Student Health Survey* (1989) assessed students' health-related knowledge, attitudes and behaviors in eight areas of critical importance to the health of youth. This survey provides a national profile of students at eighth and tenth grade levels in the areas of injury prevention; suicide; AIDS;

sexually transmitted disease (STD); violence; tobacco, alcohol and other drug use; nutrition; and consumer skills.

The Centers for Disease Control and Prevention's *Behavioral Risk Factor Survey,* established in the mid- to late-1980s, is an ongoing survey. It collects risk factor data via random digit telephone dialing. The reports, which are generated on a state-by-state basis (more than forty states are now participating), identify risk factors for disability and premature death from injury and sickness. These risk factors include tobacco, alcohol and other drug use patterns; dietary, exercise and sexual practices; safety practices such as safety belt usage, alcohol use and driving; avoidance of violence; and medical practices aimed at prevention and early detection. The risk factor survey only collects data from those households with telephones.

The *National School-Based Youth Risk Behavior Survey (YRBS)* is conducted by the Division of Adolescent and School Health of the Centers for Disease Control and Prevention. This annual school-based survey measures the prevalence of priority health-risk behaviors among students in grades nine through twelve. The YRBS focuses on priority health-risk behaviors established during adolescence that result in significant morbidity, mortality, disability and social problems among youth and adults.

The behaviors surveyed include intentional and unintentional injuries; drug and alcohol use; tobacco use; sexual behaviors that result in HIV infection, other sexually transmitted diseases (STDs) and unintended pregnancies; dietary behaviors; and physical activity. The results of this survey can be used to

- identify health-risks that your school may choose to target for reduction

- monitor how priority health-risk behaviors among high school students increase, decrease or remain the same over time

- evaluate the impact of local school efforts to prevent high-risk behaviors

- monitor the progress in objectives established by your school.

Work is currently underway to modify the questionnaire for use in surveying the health behaviors of students in grades seven and eight.

Privately Funded Surveys

Health, You've Got to Be Taught: An Evaluation of Comprehensive Health Education in American Public Schools was a national survey on the quality and effectiveness of school health education. The Metropolitan Life Foundation financed this Louis Harris survey on the knowledge, attitudes and behaviors of almost 5,000 students in grades three through twelve. The results of the survey, published in 1988, provide readers with indications of the importance young people place on different health topics, as well as their knowledge, attitudes and health behaviors. This report also includes information regarding health education currently being offered by schools and parents' perceptions of the importance of health education.

In another Louis Harris survey financed by the Metropolitan Life Foundation, *Public Attitudes Toward Teenage Pregnancy, Sex Education and Birth Control,* more than 85 percent of the adults surveyed favored sex education.

Reading the Data: Mortality and Morbidity Among Youth

The leading cause of morbidity (sickness or injury) and mortality (death) among children and young adults has been historically mislabeled as "accidents." Use of the term *accident,* which implies a random and uncontrollable event that results in injury, is widely discouraged by public health leaders. It suggests that such injuries are not preventable, when in fact many are. Most automobile crashes, for example, are neither random nor uncontrollable. More than half of all automobile-related deaths involve drivers who have been drinking. High speeds and careless driving account for the large majority of the remainder.

Such causes are preventable through education, public policy and law enforcement, behavioral changes and specific interventions. Interventions can be designed to reduce the risk factors leading to the crash, and measures can be taken to reduce the injuries that result from the crash. Table 1 shows the role injury plays in the death of children and young adults in the United States.

In the age group five to fourteen, almost half (47 percent) of all deaths are attributable to injuries. Fifty-seven percent of these deaths result from automobile crashes. More than three times as many children ages five through fourteen die from injury as from the second leading cause of death (cancers).

This trend continues in those ages fifteen to twenty-four, with 48 percent of all deaths in this age group resulting from injuries. Seventy-seven percent of these deaths result from injuries suffered in automobile crashes. And death from injury is only part of the picture. Injury that results in temporary and permanent disability to young people is more difficult to quantify, but clearly is much more frequent.

School leaders must also recognize that not all students are at equal risk of death from injuries. For example, data in Table 1 shows that boys five to fourteen years of age die at a rate almost two times that of girls of the same age. Young men ages fifteen to twenty-four die at a rate more than

Table 1

Leading Causes of Death (U.S.) for Children and Youth Ages 5–24

Rate/100,000 Population

Cause	Age 5–14			Age 15–24		
	All	Males	Females	All	Males	Females
All causes	25.8	30.9	20.4	102.1	151.0	52.1
All injury (% motor vehicle)	12.2 (57.4)	15.7 (55.4)	8.4 (61.9)	49.5 (77.8)	75.1 (75.4)	23.3 (86.3)
Homicide	1.3	1.5	1.1	15.4	24.7	6.0
Suicide	0.7	1.0	0.7	13.2	21.9	4.2
Malignant neoplasms (cancers)	3.2	3.6	2.7	5.1	5.9	4.2
Heart disease	0.9	1.1	0.8	2.9	3.8	2.1
Congenital anomalies	1.4	1.6	1.3	1.3	1.4	1.1
HIV/AIDS	—	—	—	1.4	2.4	0.5

Source: U.S. Department of Health and Human Services. 1988. *National Center for Health Statistics: Annual Report.* Washington, DC.

three times that of young women of the same age.

Other leading causes of preventable death in the fifteen- to twenty-four-year-old group include homicide, 15.4 per 100,000; suicide, 13.2 per 100,000; and HIV infection (AIDS), 1.4 per 100,000. Again, as the table indicates, young men are at greater risk of death than young women from these causes.

Deaths from cancer (5.1 per 100,000) and heart disease (2.9 per 100,000), two other leading causes of death, may not be preventable in this age group. However, certain behaviors, such as smoking, alcohol use, poor diet and lack of exercise, established by children and youth put them at risk for high rates of death and disability from heart disease and cancer in future years.

In addition to noting the inordinate risk of young men for injuries, school leaders should look for other disparities in reviewing morbidity and mortality data. Noting local or regional trends or disparities can help leaders identify and understand the risks in their particular region or student population. New Mexico has been used as an example in Table 2. These data show that although the national death rate from injuries among young men ages fifteen to twenty-four is 75.1 per 100,000, the rate among young men living in New Mexico is 109.8 per 100,000.

A similar disparity exists between the rates for young women living in New Mexico and the national rates of death from injury. School leaders may find similar geographical variances within counties, cities and even school catchment areas. It is important to consider health status and health behavior disparity between groups when planning your school-based programs.

The development of a school health education program should reflect the health status and behaviors of the children and youth in your school. Data which show the current health problems (morbidity and mortality) of children and youth, and information regarding expected future health problems (current behavioral risk factors) can help school leaders focus their health education programs. For example, an inner-city girls' school with low rates of morbidity and mortality from injury might have a different emphasis in its health education program than a suburban boys' school with high rates of death and disability from injury. The disparity in health status between groups can also provide clues to leaders interested in further investigation into potential preventive actions that can be taken to improve the health of special populations within the school.

Health status often varies between socio-economic groups as well. In general, the poorer and less educated the population, the more it experiences premature death and disability. This disparity, which results

Table 2

Leading Causes of Death (U.S. v. New Mexico) for Males Ages 5–24

Rate/100,000 Population

Cause	Age 5–14		Age 15–24	
	U.S.	New Mexico	U.S.	New Mexico
All causes	30.9	39.0	151.0	207.0
All injury (% motor vehicle)	15.7 (55.4)	22.8 (60.0)	75.1 (75.4)	109.8 (77.9)
Homicide	1.5	2.7	24.7	22.3
Suicide	1.0	1.3	21.9	48.7
Malignant neoplasms (cancers)	3.6	6.2	5.9	5.5
Heart disease	1.1	0.5	3.8	1.4
Congenital anomalies	1.6	1.1	1.4	1.7
HIV/AIDS	—	—	2.4	—

Source: New Mexico Department of Health, Public Health Division. 1989. *New Mexico Selected Health Statistics: Annual Report.* Santa Fe, New Mexico.

from the effects of poverty, insufficient opportunities and institutional inequities, is often most obvious when data is analyzed by ethnicity.

For example, Table 3 indicates that young men ages fifteen to twenty-four in New Mexico die from injury at a rate of 109.8 per 100,000. When the data is broken down by ethnicity, it shows that young White (non-Hispanic) men die at a rate of 71.3 per 100,000 and young Indian men die at a rate more than four times as great, 289.5 per 100,000.

Other areas where great disparities are apparent when the data is viewed from an ethnicity/race perspective are homicide, suicide and drug use. Epidemiologists and public health officials are wary of reporting data by ethnicity/race for fear that misunderstanding of the reasons for the disparities may result in "blaming the victims."

School leaders should use caution in interpreting ethnicity/race data. However, careful analysis of epidemiological data can guide school leaders in their efforts to develop health education programs that are specific to local community needs.

Risky Behaviors: A Better Measure of Health Status

Many experts agree that mortality and morbidity data are incomplete measures of the health of children and adolescents. Most health problems experienced by youth do not result in death (at least not immediately) and the morbidity experienced by youth—including poor health, disability due to injury, loss of educational opportunities and subsequent loss of future achievement due to teenage pregnancies, and failure to mature and develop to full potential as a result of alcohol and other drug use—is difficult to measure quantitatively.

A more relevant measure of the health status of youth is the presence or absence of health-compromising behaviors or risk factors. These unhealthy and risky behaviors, such as poor nutrition, inadequate exercise, tobacco use, early and unprotected sexual intercourse, and alcohol and other drug use, when established early in life, will eventually account for a large portion of physical and social morbidity and mortality.

For example, early and unprotected sexual intercourse results in more than one million young women ages fifteen to nineteen becoming pregnant each year. Forty percent of young women become pregnant in their teenage years, and approximately 40 percent of those pregnancies end in abortion.

These pregnancies and related abortions are the predictable results of early and unprotected sex in which youth engage. Seventy-eight percent of young women and 86 percent of young men are sexually active by age twenty.

The children of teenage mothers often

Table 3

Leading Causes of Death (New Mexico) for Males Ages 15–24 by Ethnicity/Race

Rate/100,000 Population

Cause	All races	White, non-Hispanic	Hispanic	Indian	Black*
All causes	207.0	122.2	256.5	472.4	131.3
All injury (% motor vehicle)	109.8 (77.9)	71.3 (82.0)	122.1 (77.5)	289.5 (73.7)	32.8 (66.7)
Homicide	22.3	8.2	32.2	51.8	21.9
Suicide	48.7	28.6	65.8	82.3	54.7
Malignant neoplasms (cancers)	5.5	5.3	6.2	6.1	—
Heart disease	1.4	1.8	1.4	—	—
Congenital anomalies	1.7	—	2.7	6.1	10.9
HIV/AIDS	—	—	—	—	—
Abuse of drugs	2.8	—	6.2	—	10.9

Source: New Mexico Department of Health. 1989. Public Health Division, *New Mexico Selected Health Statistics: Annual Report.* Santa Fe, New Mexico.

* The number of Blacks living in New Mexico is relatively low, which results in great variation in cause-specific mortality rates on an annual basis. Thus, caution should be exercised when viewing this data.

suffer negative health and social consequences, including low birth weight and
measurable deficiencies in health and social
development. Teenage mothers are more
likely than others to not finish school, to be
unemployed and therefore poor, and to lack
parenting skills. In addition, the negative
effects of unintended pregnancies include
emotional and psychological disruption,
social and economic problems for the mother
and her child, and negative economic
consequences for the society at large.

If school leaders, parents and community leaders share the vision of ensuring the
healthy development of children, then the
consequences of youth engaging in sex and
having babies should be viewed as social
morbidity. The burdens of this morbidity
fall directly on the shoulders of young
women.

In addition to taking action to protect
children and youth from injury and illness
in their immediate future, school-based
health programs should include efforts to
prevent the development and postpone the
onset of unhealthy and risky behaviors:

- behaviors that result in unintentional
  and intentional injuries (e.g., safety
  belt use, fighting and violence, suicide)

- use of tobacco

- use of alcohol and other drugs

- sexual behaviors that result in
  sexually transmitted disease, HIV
  infection or pregnancy

- imprudent dietary patterns

- inadequate exercise

The Iceberg of Mortality, Morbidity and
Disability (Figure 3) depicts health priority
areas identified by the U.S. Centers for
Disease Control and Prevention. Lurking
below the surface are the common factors
that contribute to the identified health
problems. These factors relate to a lack of
adequate skills to practice healthy behavior.
A comprehensive school health program can
address this lack of skills. By preparing
children to practice healthy behaviors, it
enhances their skills for life.

Educational and Behaviorial Research—Promoting Health

A great many programs have been developed and implemented to prevent the
development of specific health problems in
youth. There is a growing consensus about
what these efforts should include. In some
cases, evaluation provides evidence to support
this consensus. The main points are these:

- Accurate information about students'
  current knowledge, skills and practices serves as a basis for planning
  instruction that meets the needs of
  students.

- The relationship among knowledge,
  skills and behavior has important
  implications for education and

Figure 3

The Iceberg of Mortality, Morbidity and Disability[1]

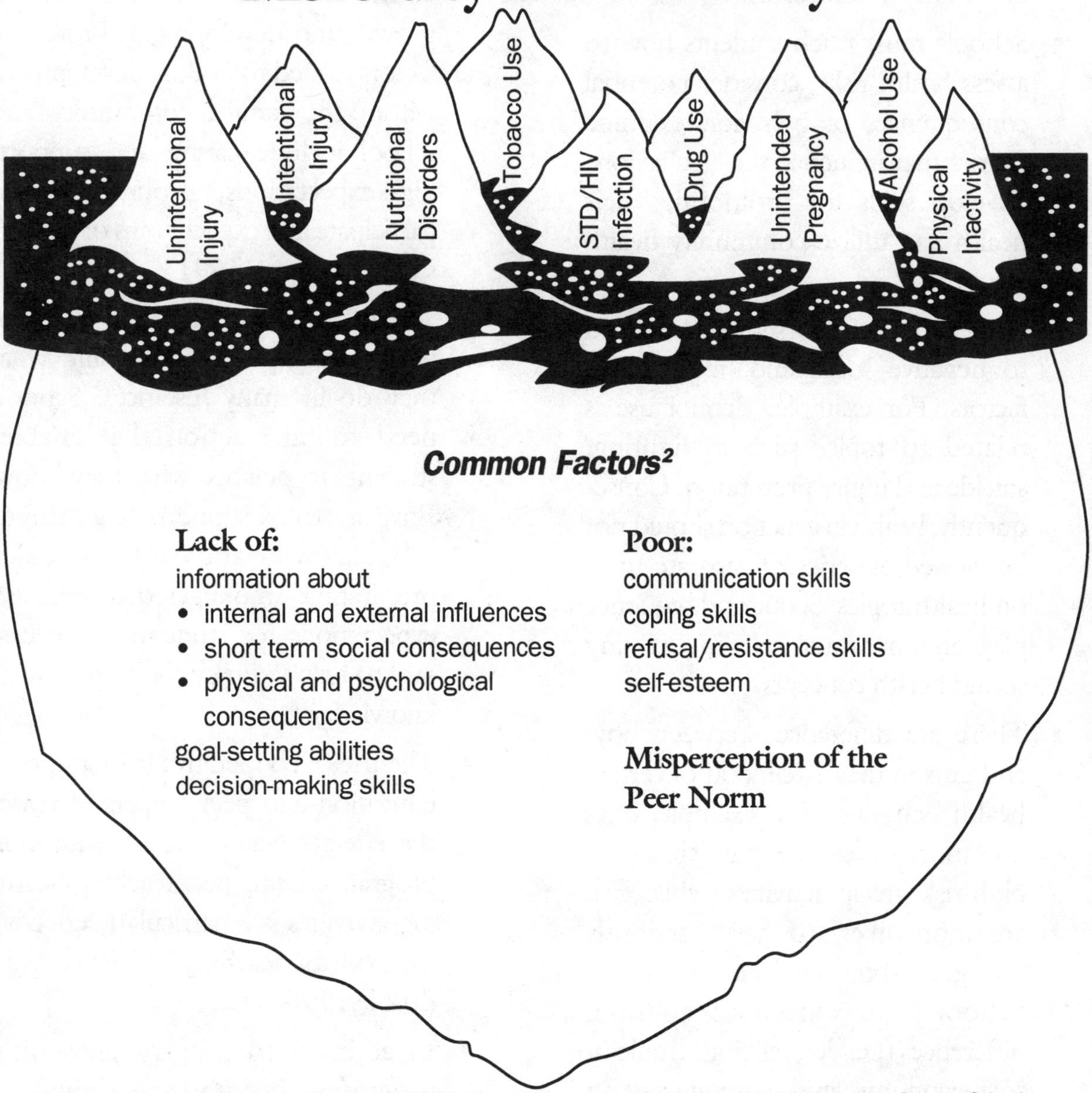

Unintentional Injury

Intentional Injury

Nutritional Disorders

Tobacco Use

STD/HIV Infection

Drug Use

Unintended Pregnancy

Alcohol Use

Physical Inactivity

Common Factors[2]

Lack of:
information about
• internal and external influences
• short term social consequences
• physical and psychological consequences
goal-setting abilities
decision-making skills

Poor:
communication skills
coping skills
refusal/resistance skills
self-esteem

Misperception of the Peer Norm

[1]Centers for Disease Control and Prevention. 1991. Program Announcement, Cooperative Agreements to Support School Health Education to Prevent the Spread of HIV and Other Important Health Problems.
[2]Fetro, J.V. 1992. *Personal and Social Skills: Understanding and Integrating Competencies Across Health Content.* Santa Cruz, CA: ETR Associates.

attitudes about health. Instruction must be concerned not only with knowledge, but with skills and behaviors that lead to the development of healthy attitudes.

- Schools must teach students how to assess health risks, consider potential consequences of behavior, examine factors that influence their behaviors, develop skills for promoting their health and utilize community health resources.

- Unhealthy behaviors can be related to negative social and health-status factors. For example, alcohol use is related to topics such as fighting, suicide and injury prevention. Consequently, health instruction should not be viewed as series of separate units on health topics. Scope and sequence play an important role in building sound health concepts.

- There are differences between boys and girls in their likelihood of certain health behaviors. For example, boys are more likely to participate in high-risk group activities, while girls are more likely to have "seriously thought" about committing suicide. School leaders need to consider differences (gender, religion, ethnicity, socioeconomic level) among students in planning for health education.

- High expectations, a sense of purpose and future, problem-solving skills and the ability to act independently have been identified as factors that protect youth and facilitate their healthy growth and development. Protective factors related to healthy development within the family, community and school include caring and support, high expectations, encouragement to participate and expectations of responsibility (Benard, 1991).

- There are inconsistencies between what young people know and what they do in many instances. Schools need to take action that enables students to practice what they know. Environmental supports (e.g., parental curfews and school rules prohibiting smoking) that establish expectations for students are necessary to help young people apply their knowledge.

- The use of cooperative learning, peer education and peer helpers increases the effectiveness of health education programs. Using peer teaching/learning activities is a particularly effective method for teaching resistance skills (Tobler, 1986).

- In addition to primary prevention programs (programs designed to prevent the onset of risky behaviors), student assistance programs that provide for early identification of unhealthy behaviors and early intervention are important components of the overall school health program (Berdiansky, McKinney and Richardson, 1992).

- Problems identified in schools, such as drugs and violence, are not confined to school settings; they are family and community problems as well. Therefore, schools, families and community as well as children benefit from collaborative efforts to address adolescent health problems (ASHA, AAHE and SOPHE, 1989).

- Preventive efforts that use comprehensive approaches involving multiple systems and addressing multiple issues may be more effective than traditional single-issue, single-focus approaches (U.S. Congress, 1991).

- Knowledge alone is not sufficient for adolescents to make healthy choices. Skills, opportunities and reinforcement for the practice of healthy behaviors must be available (ASHA, AAHE and SOPHE).

- Preventive efforts that change environments (e.g., safety belts and air bags that provide automatic protection in auto crashes) are an essential component of overall prevention efforts (U.S. Congress).

- Preventive efforts that provide students with some form of concrete aid (e.g., contraceptive devices) or improved competencies (e.g., life-skills training) are more effective primary prevention strategies than strictly didactic, education-based interventions (U.S. Congress).

- Health education works best when it includes teacher training and integrated materials, when it is implemented with continuity across grades, and when it builds on a foundation of basic health knowledge.

- The effectiveness of school health education increases with increased time spent on instruction. Figure 4 shows the relationship of effect size and instruction hours for health knowledge, practices and attitudes.

School leaders responsible for creating school-based health education programs are often overwhelmed by the magnitude of the task. How does the school help children and youth acquire health awareness and knowledge and develop skills, provide opportunities to practice these skills, and reinforce students for healthy behaviors? An equally important question is, How does the school interact with the family and community in each of these areas to maximize the chances that students will adopt healthy behaviors, which will in turn lead to the establishment of healthful norms in the school, home and community? And how does all of this fit within the ten priority

health content areas identified by leaders in the health field?

Figure 5 provides an illustration of the relationship between these various factors.

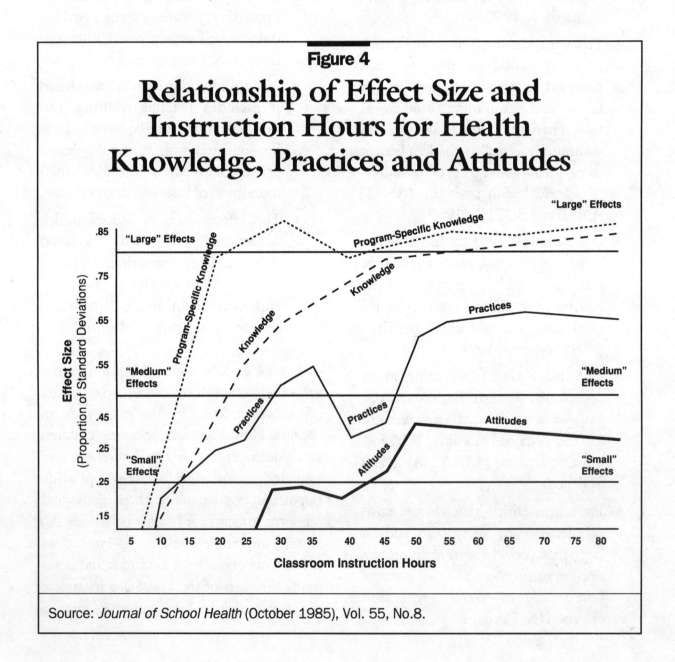

Figure 4
Relationship of Effect Size and Instruction Hours for Health Knowledge, Practices and Attitudes

Source: *Journal of School Health* (October 1985), Vol. 55, No.8.

The wheel depicts the healthy student at the center, as the focal point of classroom, school, home (family) and community efforts to promote health. The spokes of the wheel represent the ingredients that enable students to adopt healthy behaviors. These are awareness and knowledge of health issues, skills necessary to practice healthy behaviors, opportunities to practice healthy behaviors, planned reinforcement for healthy behaviors, and the adoption of healthful norms by the school, families and community to provide an environment of support. Given health awareness, health knowledge, health skills and an opportunity to practice healthy behaviors, children and youth will be more likely to adopt and incorporate healthy behaviors as lifestyle habits.

The subsequent value which peers, school leaders, family and community members place on healthy behaviors (healthful norms) reinforces positive self-concepts and produces positive attitudes toward the practice of healthy behaviors. The increasing or decreasing width of the spokes as they pass through the rings—classroom, school, home and community—indicate the role each environment has in providing leadership in each area. For example, the school plays a major role in helping children and youth acquire awareness and knowledge and develop skills to practice healthy behaviors.

On the other hand, the greatest opportunities to practice healthy behaviors exist in the community. The ability of children and youth to practice healthy behaviors in the unrestricted environment of the community is the real test of the success of a health education program. For example, does a 15 year old refuse to ride in an automobile with a friend who has been drinking?

Children and youth can apply their knowledge and skills to situations that involve traditional content areas such as nutrition, disease prevention, substance use prevention and injury prevention. Figure 5 shows this relationship by placing the content areas on the outside of the community environment.

Properly designed school-based health education programs help children and youth acquire the necessary awareness, knowledge and health-related skills, and provide opportunities within the classroom and school for students to practice healthy behaviors. Quality school programs also recognize that the family and community play an important role in students' learning and provide wider opportunities to practice and reinforce healthy behaviors. School health education programs that are committed to working with families and communities to provide health education, health and social services, and an environment that promotes and rewards healthy behaviors will be taking an important step in supporting the healthy development of children and youth. This is the goal of comprehensive school health efforts.

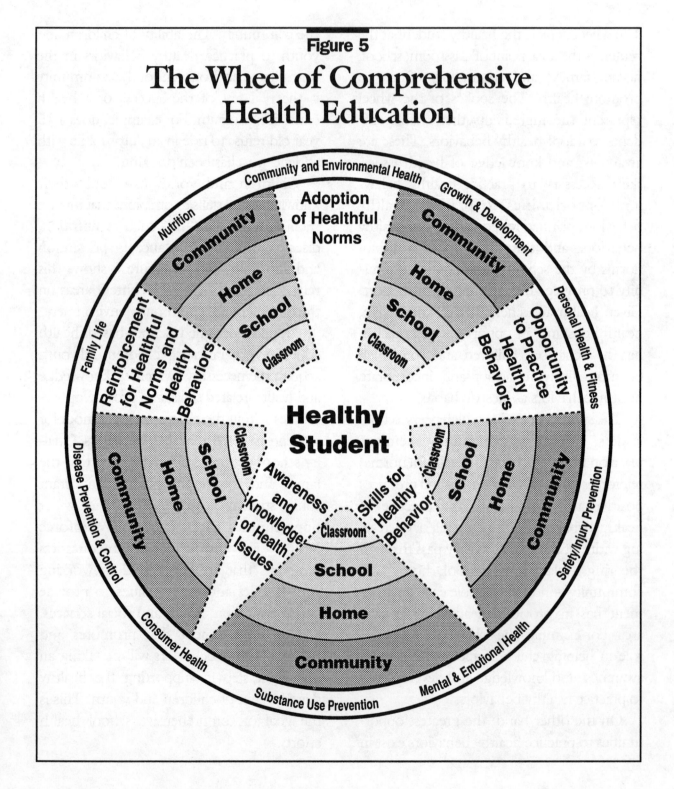

Figure 5

The Wheel of Comprehensive Health Education

2

A Blueprint for School Health Programs

The school's role in fostering the healthy development of children and youth goes beyond the teacher providing health education in class. Although health education (instruction) is a critical component in a child's healthy development, there are other efforts the school should undertake to support the healthy development of children.

Allensworth and Kolbe (1987) provide a useful overall framework for thinking about a comprehensive approach to promote the health of school-age children and youth. Their framework identifies eight components of schools that can be organized and combined to create a comprehensive program:

- school health education (instruction)
- healthy school environment
- school health services
- school-based physical education

- school nutrition and food services
- school-based counseling and personal support
- schoolsite health promotion
- school, family and community health promotion partnerships

This section describes each of these components, identifies opportunities within each component to enhance the health of students, and provides assessment worksheets. The worksheets can be used by school leaders to evaluate the opportunities that currently exist to promote the health of students. This information can help school leaders develop a snapshot of the school's current efforts, identify and capitalize on potential opportunities to promote the health of students, and determine the direction of future efforts.

School Health Education (Instruction)

School health education or instruction is a combination of educational activities with the following aims:

- to increase students' health knowledge
- to develop health-promoting skills
- to provide opportunities for the application of health knowledge and skills
- to reinforce and foster the continued practice of healthy behaviors

The end goal of school health education (instruction) is to give individuals the knowledge, skills, opportunities and support to develop to their fullest potential. School health education should be based on a planned and sequential curriculum that interacts with the other components of the comprehensive health program to enable young people to achieve optimal health. (Appendix C provides a sample scope and sequence for a comprehensive school health program.)

The curriculum is planned in that it should be based on the current documentable threats to the health of young people. School leaders can look to national, state and local morbidity and mortality statistics for some of this data. Behavioral risk-factor data that identifies behaviors that put youth

at increased risk of future health problems are also available from the U.S. Centers for Disease Control and Prevention and state departments of health.

The aspirations of families and communities, as well as the hopes of the students themselves, are also important foundations upon which to develop health curricula. Successful school health education programs involve a wide range of individuals, including:

- students and their families
- community members
- representatives of business, health and social service professions
- clergy
- community leaders

All of these people should be represented in the process of planning a curriculum that is appropriate and sensitive to the cultural needs of the community and school. A health education curriculum that represents a collectively shared vision of the importance of the health of children is the first step toward helping all children develop to their optimal health potential.

Curriculum Content

Although school districts often have different names for the content areas of their particular curriculum, the range of topics included in most school health curricula can be grouped into the following ten areas:

Prevention of alcohol and other drug use: Includes the beneficial and appropriate use of drugs and medications, as well as the harmful and inappropriate uses; reasons why people do not use drugs; techniques for avoiding drug use; and methods for resisting a wide range of societal pressures to use drugs.

Nutrition and healthy eating: Deals with the importance of healthy food for body growth and development; components of a healthy diet; nutritional quality of food; differing nutritional needs of people of various ages, body types and activity levels; healthy food selection and preparation; nutrition and body composition; nutrition and chronic disease prevention; and eating to maintain optimal health.

Family life education: Includes the roles, relationships and interactions of family members; the responsibilities and privileges of being part of a family; the physical, mental and social progression through the life cycle; communications and negotiations within the family.

Mental and emotional health: Looks at individual development of a sense of self in relation to others; social awareness and self-concept; identifying, understanding, managing and communicating emotions; applying problem-solving skills; respecting others; and accepting personal responsibility for one's own health.

Environmental health: Examines the relationship between environment and personal health; effects of environment on physical and mental/emotional health; conservation of natural resources and prevention of environmental pollution; and accepting personal responsibility for working to preserve the environment for future generations.

Injury prevention and safety: Includes assessing risks and identifying potential hazards and threats to personal safety; planning ahead for safety; use of special safety equipment; purpose of safety rules; safe friends; and avoiding risky behaviors.

Personal health and fitness: Deals with the development of healthy self-care and healthy actions that promote overall wellness and physical fitness and physical health over the life span.

Disease prevention and control: Includes identification of levels of health and illness; personal assessment of health status and determining need for expert medical attention; and personal and collective actions to prevent and control infectious and chronic disease.

Community health: Examines character-istics of healthy communities; personal responsibility for health of community; individuals as health advocates; health workers; health agencies; and career opportunities.

Selecting health options (consumer health): Includes identifying, evaluating and select-ing healthy products; securing appropriate health-promoting, diagnostic and treatment services; evaluating health claims; recognizing forces that are used to promote products and services; and decision making related to health choices.

All ten content areas are not covered at each grade level. Decisions regarding the scope and focus of the curriculum at each grade level are based on what is appropriate to the interests, needs and physical and mental development of students. The health education curriculum and content should be sequential, each year building on and reinforcing the knowledge learned and the skills developed at earlier grade levels.

Health Skills

Health education curricula include both content and process. The process, or *skills development*, is the major focus of the curriculum and the classroom activities. These health-related skills are defined a bit

differently by each school district, but fall into the following general categories.

Assessing Personal Health and Risks

Before students can take action to protect themselves from risks to health and safety, they need to have knowledge about them-selves personally, in addition to knowledge about potential risks related to a behavior. Students also need the skills to assess health risks and the ability to perceive themselves at risk. Other skills important to risk assess-ment include:

- assessing personal strengths and weaknesses
- identifying personal likes and dislikes
- gathering information
- evaluating information
- identifying internal and external influences on behavior
- identifying potential and immediate dangers
- identifying future consequences of actions
- assessing the availability of resources

Gathering and Assessing Health Information

Locating sources of health information, accessing that information and evaluating the validity of the information are all critical to enabling individuals to take healthy action. Subskills important to the development and successful practice of gathering and assessing health information include:

- identifying possible sources of health information
- accessing information
- listening and processing verbal interchanges
- comprehending written material
- evaluating information
- comparing information from various sources
- validating information with one's personal sense of reality

Rewarding Healthy Behavior

Students' ability to sustain the practice of healthy behavior is in large part dependent on their perceiving successful results when that behavior is practiced. Feeling good about a behavior increases the likelihood that an individual will continue to practice the behavior. Students can be taught to reward themselves for their behaviors. Students, teachers, school administrators, family members and others can learn to provide reinforcement for the healthy behaviors of others. That reinforcement could be praise or some more tangible reward

(e.g., allowance) earned for practicing healthy behavior. Subskills necessary to provide reinforcement include:

- assessing personal likes and preferences
- articulating preferences
- clarifying issues of importance to others
- identifying opportunities to reward oneself and others
- delivering rewards in acceptable ways
- developing personal relationships with others

Communicating with Others

Communication is an essential prevention skill. Students who have developed effective communication skills can establish a feeling of connectiveness; express their feelings, needs and desires; communicate their health needs; reinforce the healthy behaviors of others; and resist internal or external pressures to practice unhealthy behaviors. Subskills necessary for communication include:

- initiating conversation
- expressing oneself verbally and nonverbally
- listening, processing and clarifying verbal and nonverbal communications
- responding to verbal and nonverbal requests

- accepting differences in oneself and others
- identifying potential barriers to communication

Making Decisions

When combined with health knowledge and the opportunity to make healthy choices, the ability to make decisions is a powerful skill. Students need to be able to identify decision points, clarify complex issues, gather information, evaluate the advantages and disadvantages of alternatives and take action. This ability moves students one step closer to good health. Subskills necessary for making decisions include:

- recognizing when decisions are needed
- gathering and organizing information
- identifying decisions that one is responsible for and capable of making
- analyzing complex issues
- identifying alternatives
- relating personal and family values to alternatives
- identifying possible positive and negative consequences of actions
- analyzing options
- choosing a course of action
- evaluating decisions and making changes

Negotiating for Health

Pressure from peers, societal norms and the influence of advertising are often in conflict with personal, family and cultural norms and the practice of healthy behavior. Students need to be able to negotiate the right and the opportunities to practice healthy behaviors. Negotiating for health is more than communicating what you want; it involves resisting pressures to choose options that are inconsistent with personal, family or cultural values. Skills essential to negotiating for health include:

- clarifying personal beliefs and values
- articulating personal, family and cultural beliefs and needs
- listening to new ideas and options
- evaluating and considering options
- resisting pressures from others
- resolving conflicts
- refuting arguments of others
- acting on one's beliefs and desires
- being open and prepared to compromise

Managing Stress

Stress is part of everyone's daily routine. Although we commonly think of stress as a result of negative events, stress also results from positive events. The ability to deal with stressful situations without harming one's health is an essential skill. Students need to be able to identify situations that create stress and understand how to minimize its potentially harmful effects. Skills necessary for managing stress include:

- identifying/recognizing situations that create stress
- planning ahead to avoid stress
- clarifying personal expectations
- maintaining high levels of fitness and nutrition
- anticipating and planning to avoid future stressors
- making accommodations to change
- coping strategies (relaxing, exercise, meditation, hobbies, etc.)
- establishing and maintaining social support systems
- securing help from health professionals
- reassessing situations to alter one's perception of stressors

Setting and Achieving Goals

The ability to set and achieve goals is important to practicing healthy behavior. Students who can identify their needs, set goals and take action to achieve those goals are able to take charge of creating their own opportunities to practice healthy behaviors. Skills necessary for setting and achieving goals include:

- assessing personal needs, strengths and weaknesses
- assessing the availability of resources
- clarifying personal expectations
- identifying decisions and steps for achieving goals
- projecting future scenarios (short-term and long-term)
- identifying possible consequences of future actions
- reducing complex tasks to simple components
- initiating specific action

School leaders will want to develop a curriculum that provides learning opportunities for students to acquire awareness and knowledge regarding health; skills and opportunities to practice healthy behaviors; and encouragement and reinforcement for developing healthy lifestyles. A curriculum of this type relies heavily on experiential learning.

Unlike curricula in many other areas, a health curriculum is constantly in a state of change, reflecting developments in culture, society, technology and behavioral sciences. An annual review should be conducted to determine the relevance of the present curriculum to the priorities and needs of the local community.

Instructional Time

Planning for instructional time is another important issue school leaders will want to consider in developing the school health education program. Most authorities recommend that elementary and middle school students experience the equivalent of two to three hours of health education each week. Integration of health education learning experiences into other, subject-oriented learning experiences can be successfully accomplished.

However, experience shows that many schools that report use of the integrated approach are not successful in helping students gain the knowledge or develop the skills or in providing the opportunities to practice healthy behaviors. This lack of success may be due not to the integrated approach, but to the level of commitment, time and priority that the teachers and school place on quality health instruction. Many leaders recommend that elementary schools establish specific times for health instruction as well as integrate health education into other subjects in the curriculum.

Health education should continue beyond elementary school. Early adolescence is a critical time; young people are exploring various behaviors, making choices and establishing life-long health behaviors. Health education in grades seven and eight should include sixty to seventy hours of direct instruction and learning experiences each year. At the high school level, students should be encouraged to include at least two semesters of health instruction in their schedules.

Teacher Skills and Preparation

The skills and preparation of the classroom teacher are critical to the success of school health education. Teachers should be professionally prepared, through preservice and inservice education, to implement the health curriculum, to foster health-related learning, to help students develop health and life skills, and to work with the school, families and community to provide opportunities to practice healthy behavior.

Teachers should keep in mind that the health needs and interests of their students will differ from student to student, from class to class, from community to community and from culture to culture. The optimal school health education program will allow the skilled teacher to modify learning opportunities accordingly.

Teachers should be fully prepared in the following areas:

- handling controversial health issues and content

- experiential learning

- peer education, cooperative learning and cross-tutoring

- strategies to foster development of critical thinking
- health counseling
- family relations and counseling
- advocacy
- life-skills training
- rewarding healthy behavior
- modeling healthy behavior

Administrative Leadership

Administrative leadership in allocating instructional time and providing policy, funding and support for training and materials to implement successful health education programs is also important. School leaders have a responsibility to work with their communities, initiating action and providing leadership in policy and funding areas. Administrators are also responsible for implementation of programs and follow-up once a program is in place.

Instructional Materials

Instructional and educational materials for health instruction include a wide range of textbooks, prepackaged curricula, supplementary texts, videos and materials that can be used in conjunction with local and state-developed curriculum or commercial curricula. (See Appendix D for a list of organizations that publish health education materials.)

Worksheet 1 can be used to evaluate the current health education (instruction) provided in your school.

Healthy School Environment

A safe and healthy environment is important for education. Schools should not be places where students and teachers fear for their personal safety. Harassment from gang members and drug pushers and resolution of conflict by violent actions has no place in the school.

Commitment to regular safety inspections, emergency drills, safe and orderly transportation, adherence to environmental regulations and standards, and clean, safe and well-maintained school grounds and buildings communicate a message to all by establishing health norms and expectations. The physical surroundings in which students and teachers are expected to work should promote healthy behaviors.

Likewise, students' personal achievements and social growth are fostered by the psychological environment of the school. Teachers serve as health role models for their students. The emotional and physical health and the social, problem-solving and conflict-management skills demonstrated by

Worksheet 1

School Health Education

How established are the following aspects of comprehensive school health education in your school?

Established
Not — Well

A "vision" for school health education that is clearly stated, widely accepted and commonly shared 1 2 3 4 5 6 7

Curriculum advisory committee with representation from health professionals, civic leaders, family members and students 1 2 3 4 5 6 7

Curriculum based on epidemiological diagnosis of the health problems of school-age children 1 2 3 4 5 6 7

Curriculum that reflects the priorities of the local community 1 2 3 4 5 6 7

Curriculum that builds sequentially throughout the grades 1 2 3 4 5 6 7

Curriculum that, overall, addresses all the ten content areas for health education 1 2 3 4 5 6 7

Curriculum that includes a focus on health skills development 1 2 3 4 5 6 7

Curriculum that includes a focus on providing students the opportunities to practice the knowledge and skills learned in the classroom 1 2 3 4 5 6 7

Curriculum that includes learning activities to involve family members and community experiences 1 2 3 4 5 6 7

A process that facilitates a routine annual review of the curriculum.........................1 2 3 4 5 6 7

Teachers prepared to implement health education 1 2 3 4 5 6 7

Routine health education inservice to strengthen teachers' skills and keep knowledge up to date 1 2 3 4 5 6 7

Adequate budget for health education curricular materials, teaching supplies, inservice education and supervision 1 2 3 4 5 6 7

Two to three hours of health instruction weekly in each elementary grade 1 2 3 4 5 6 7

Sixty to seventy hours of health instruction in each of grades seven and eight 1 2 3 4 5 6 7

Two semesters of health education at the high school level....................1 2 3 4 5 6 7

Sufficient material to support the curriculum and teachers in class instruction 1 2 3 4 5 6 7

Formal mechanisms for integrating classroom instruction with the other comprehensive school health program components 1 2 3 4 5 6 7

Ongoing opportunities for community members to be involved in planning and instruction 1 2 3 4 5 6 7

Total School Health Education Score: ____/133

teachers influence young people.

Not surprisingly, research has found that among the reported positive role models in the lives of many people is a favorite teacher. Teachers are not only developers of academic skills, but also positive models for students' personal identification and development.

The health norms and social expectations created by the school act as a factor to support healthy development of students. Benard (1991) has identified the level of caring and support within the school as a powerful predictor of positive outcomes for youth.

Researchers have concluded that schools that are successful in helping young people overcome problem behaviors project clear expectations and regulations, emphasize academics, have high levels of student participation, foster high self-esteem, and promote social and scholastic success. Schools that establish high expectations for all students and provide the support necessary to achieve these expectations have high rates of academic success.

Benard's review of the research on the school's role in developing resilient youth concludes that the caregiving environment of the school can serve as a protective shield in reducing levels of alcohol and other drug use.

"At a time when the traditional structures of caring have deteriorated, schools must become places where teachers and students live together, talk with each other, take delight in each other's company...children will work harder for people they love and trust" (Noddings, 1988).

Are you providing safe and healthy schools that foster the physical, emotional, social and academic development of the children of your community? Worksheet 2 will allow you to evaluate the current healthy vitality of your school environment. Your initial assessment can be used as baseline data and serve as a beginning point. Unmet needs can be identified, and opportunities and strategies for enhancing your school's health-promoting environment can be formulated.

Using the worksheet periodically and comparing scores on an annual basis will enable the school to evaluate its efforts to provide a safe and healthy environment for student learning and development. School leaders may wish to seek input from community leaders and students' parents and families regarding their perceptions of the school environment.

School Health Services

The provision of health services by schools emerged near the end of the nineteenth century in response to compulsory education laws. The focus of these services was to prevent and control infectious diseases and

School Environment

How established are your school site's *emergency procedures* for taking quick action to assert control of playgrounds, schoolyards and buildings in the following situations?

Established
Not — Well

Gang member disruptions 1 2 3 4 5 6 7

Drug-related situations (i.e., selling, buying, possession, overdose) 1 2 3 4 5 6 7

Bomb scares, terrorists, weapons on campus 1 2 3 4 5 6 7

Fires, earthquakes, gas leaks, other unexpected mishaps 1 2 3 4 5 6 7

Death of a student or staff member 1 2 3 4 5 6 7

Suicide of a student, staff member or prominent community member 1 2 3 4 5 6 7

Emergency Procedures Score: ___/42

How adequate is your school district's *emergency communication system* in the following areas?

Adequate
Not — Very

Classroom to classroom 1 2 3 4 5 6 7

Classroom to office 1 2 3 4 5 6 7

Office to buses 1 2 3 4 5 6 7

School to district office 1 2 3 4 5 6 7

School to other schools 1 2 3 4 5 6 7

School to police 1 2 3 4 5 6 7

School to fire department 1 2 3 4 5 6 7

School to electric company 1 2 3 4 5 6 7

School to paramedics 1 2 3 4 5 6 7

School to disaster center 1 2 3 4 5 6 7

Emergency Communications Score: ___/70

Worksheet 2 continued

Does your school have policies and procedures for handling the following situations?

*Established
Not — Well*

Sale and possession of alcohol and other drugs 1 2 3 4 5 6 7

Possession of weapons (guns, knives, etc.) 1 2 3 4 5 6 7

Universal precautions for handling blood and other body fluids..............1 2 3 4 5 6 7

Tobacco use by students and staff on campus 1 2 3 4 5 6 7

Physical violence 1 2 3 4 5 6 7

Policy Score: ____/35

How would you rate your school's emphasis on the following *health and safety* areas?

*Emphasis
Low — High*

Sanitation, lighting, heat control, trash, noise control...............................1 2 3 4 5 6 7

Cleanliness, attractiveness, landscaping 1 2 3 4 5 6 7

Compliance with and establishment of health and safety policies and procedures 1 2 3 4 5 6 7

Protection of students and teachers from violence, drug pushers,
unwelcome visitors and harassment 1 2 3 4 5 6 7

Health and Safety Score: ____/28

Worksheet 2 continued

What emphasis does your school place on activities to promote positive health?

Emphasis
Low — High

Involving students in promoting a healthy school environment 1 2 3 4 5 6 7

Displaying creative work of students 1 2 3 4 5 6 7

Empowering teachers to be healthy physical, social and emotional role models 1 2 3 4 5 6 7

Establishing high expectations for all students 1 2 3 4 5 6 7

Fostering high self-esteem 1 2 3 4 5 6 7

Promoting social and scholastic success 1 2 3 4 5 6 7

Providing students opportunities to participate and have responsible roles
within the school 1 2 3 4 5 6 7

Providing opportunities for students to practice healthy behaviors 1 2 3 4 5 6 7

Reinforcing healthy behaviors of students and teachers 1 2 3 4 5 6 7

Caring for and supporting students and teachers 1 2 3 4 5 6 7

Health Promotion Score: ____/70

Total Healthy School Environment Score: ____/245

exclude those children who represented a health threat to others.

Much has changed over the past hundred years. The 1990 Joint Committee on Health Education Terminology's definition of school health services identified school health services personnel and their responsibilities. School health service personnel include the following individuals who appraise, protect and promote the health of students and school personnel:

- physicians
- nurses
- dentists
- health educators
- allied health personnel
- social workers
- teachers

The definition goes on to describe school health services as those activities designed to

- insure access to and appropriate use of primary health care services
- prevent and control communicable disease
- provide emergency care for injury or sudden illness
- promote and provide optimum sanitary conditions in a safe school facility and environment
- provide concurrent learning opportunities conducive to the maintenance

and promotion of individual and community health

For example, health services provided by the school and community to all students in one Massachusetts school district include:

- immunizations
- vision and hearing screening
- fluoride dental rinse program
- dental screening, sealants and cavity repair
- physical evaluation
- speech therapy
- postural screening
- pediculosis (body lice) screening
- health assessment and individual education plans
- child abuse assessment
- prekindergarten and kindergarten screening
- management of asthmatics
- mental health counseling and referral
- family outreach/parent support groups
- inservice education for staff
- supplemental health education in classrooms

School leaders need to delineate the difference between school health services and health services for school-age children.

School health services function to support the process of education and ensure that children are healthy enough to participate in the educational process. School health services were never intended to replace the existing health care delivery system of the community. They are, however, often the best location for providing collaborative services by other community agencies.

School nurses have traditionally been the focal point for health services in the schools. In addition, school nurses are a key resource for the other components of the overall school health program, as they provide health education and act as consultants on community and family health.

Unfortunately, there are only about thirty thousand school nurses throughout the country to serve nearly 42 million students. The National School Nurses Association recommends a ratio of one nurse for every 750 students. To achieve this ratio, we would need more than twenty thousand additional school nurses. In the absence of adequate funding for school nurses, many schools rely on a school secretary to administer first-aid and minor medications.

A recent report of the Carnegie Council on Adolescent Development called for all schools to establish a health coordinator whose principle task is to marshal available health care resources on behalf of students. As a result of the rapidly escalating costs of health care, combined with today's unstable market for employment, many adults and their children have no medical insurance and limited access to primary health care. Many schools (and communities) are now exploring alternative methods of providing health services for young people.

More than one hundred health clinics based in schools have emerged over the past decade. These clinics provide a full range of primary health care services and act as a point of referral for students requiring more extensive diagnostic work, treatment and rehabilitation.

Unfortunately, many of these clinics have become embroiled in controversy surrounding the provision of sexuality counseling and birth control devices. By the end of high school (grades 9–12), 60.8 percent of males and 48 percent of females report they have had sexual intercourse (U.S. Department of Health and Human Services, 1990). About 60,000 babies are born each year to adolescent girls under fifteen years of age.

Family planning counseling and provision of services are appropriate roles for school-based clinics. School-based clinics are proving both effective and expensive. Efforts to establish school-based clinics will require that school leaders secure cooperation and support from existing community health care providers and the local public health unit.

Some schools (and communities) are experimenting with health insurance coverage for students. Actually, the concept of accident insurance for students has been around for decades. Today's student health insurance has been expanded to cover regular check-ups, immunizations, hospitalizations, outpatient care, prescriptions, eye glasses, and drug and alcohol treatment and rehabilitation. These insurance plans are being financed through community fundraising, public health agencies and private insurance carriers.

In every school, the physical and mental health needs of some students will exceed the immediate resources of the school and its personnel. Paying for health care is an expensive and complex societal issue. However, good health is essential for learning and for achieving one's fullest potential. School leaders need to work closely with families, community leaders and health and social service providers to establish a systematic health care system for children.

Worksheet 3 enables you to assess your school's current health services.

School-Based Physical Education

It is widely held that participation in physical education activities promotes health development. More than 97 percent of this country's elementary school children and 80 percent of its secondary school students have access to organized physical education.

Students in elementary schools take physical education an average of 3.1 times weekly, with 36.4 percent taking classes daily. At the high school level, students take physical education an average of 3.9 times weekly, with 36.3 percent taking classes daily (Office of Disease Prevention and Health Promotion, 1984).

The popular literature attributes a large range of benefits to physical exercise, including:

- improved cardiovascular and physiological functioning
- reduction of stress
- reduction of weight and body fat
- improved skeletal and muscle structure
- increased sense of self-worth
- improved academic performance

Indeed, research findings seem to support many of these popular beliefs. Yet despite the growing body of knowledge regarding the effects of physical fitness and exercise on health and the long existence of physical education programs in America's schools, all is not well. The *National Children and Youth Fitness Study* released in 1984 cited the following problems:

- Body fat of today's youth is significantly greater than in the 1960s.
- Only 50 percent of today's youth

Worksheet 3

School Health Services

What school health services does your school provide?

Established
Not — Well

Secures a health status profile on each student entering school. 1 2 3 4 5 6 7

Maintains a current up-to-date health record on all enrolled students. 1 2 3 4 5 6 7

Ensures childhood immunization for admittance to school. 1 2 3 4 5 6 7

Provides for routine vision and hearing screening for all students. 1 2 3 4 5 6 7

Provides for mental health evaluations, counseling and referral. 1 2 3 4 5 6 7

Provides for dental health screening and referral. 1 2 3 4 5 6 7

Provides fluoridated dental rinse, toothbrushes, toothpaste and
dental floss for students. 1 2 3 4 5 6 7

Ensures that all students have access to physical and mental health
and dental care. 1 2 3 4 5 6 7

Provides emergency care for injury and sudden illness. 1 2 3 4 5 6 7

Systematically alerts teachers regarding student health issues that
may require special educational considerations. 1 2 3 4 5 6 7

Provides assistance to all teachers in preparing individual educational
programs to meet unique health needs of students. 1 2 3 4 5 6 7

Coordinates management of special health needs of students
during school hours. 1 2 3 4 5 6 7

Provides speech therapy for students. 1 2 3 4 5 6 7

Ensures rapid health and legal response in cases of possible child abuse. 1 2 3 4 5 6 7

Has a system for teachers' referral of suspected health problems. 1 2 3 4 5 6 7

Has a system for diagnosis, referral, treatment and rehabilitation
of student health problems. 1 2 3 4 5 6 7

Provides inservice for teachers and staff to help them identify, refer and
manage students with special health needs. 1 2 3 4 5 6 7

Has a mechanism established for routinely meeting with community
health care providers to discuss health care for children. 1 2 3 4 5 6 7

Encourages abstinence and provides family planning counseling and
services for students. 1 2 3 4 5 6 7

Has a mechanism for securing health care for families of students. 1 2 3 4 5 6 7

All students can secure routine health care services. 1 2 3 4 5 6 7

Total School Health Services Score: ___/147

participate in appropriate physical activity.

- Only 50 percent of the students in twelfth grade participate in physical education classes.

- Physical education teachers devote most classroom time to competitive sports and other activities that have questionable health effects and that cannot readily be performed once one reaches adulthood.

Recognizing the importance of exercise, the U.S. Department of Health and Human Services' *Healthy People 2000* recommends that by the year 2000 "schools increase by at least 50 percent [baseline 36 percent in 1984–86] the proportion of children and adolescents in 1st through 12th grade who participate in daily school physical education" (Objective #1.8). In 1987, both houses of Congress passed a resolution encouraging state and local educational agencies to provide high quality daily physical education programs for all children in kindergarten through twelfth grade. Only one state, Illinois, currently requires daily physical education as part of the curriculum in kindergarten through twelfth grade.

The proportion of students participating in daily physical education is one measure of the quality of school-based physical education. Other measures of quality identified by

Healthy People 2000 are students' exposure to information about how and why to partake in activities and encouragement of students to develop skills that allow for out-of-school and lifetime activities.

Lifetime physical activities are defined as those activities in which an individual can participate throughout his or her life. These include tennis, badminton, golf, hiking, individual exercise, swimming and bicycling. They do not include football, soccer, baseball, basketball or most competitive team activities that commonly dominate the high school curriculum.

Healthy People 2000 recommends that by the year 2000 we "increase to at least 50 percent [baseline 27 percent in 1984] the proportion of school physical education class time that students spend being physically active, preferably engaged in lifetime physical activities" (Objective #1.9). Studies indicate that only 27 percent of the current physical education classroom time is spent in actual physical activity, while 26 percent is spent in instruction, 22 percent is spent in administrative tasks and 25 percent is spent waiting.

Physical education is another area of the school health program that requires coordination between schools, families and communities. The typical student in fifth through twelfth grades reports that more than 80 percent of his or her physical activity takes place outside of physical education classes. The majority of this time is spent in activities sponsored by community organizations, including religious groups, parks and recreation programs, local teams and private organizations.

The variety and type of activity these young people engage in varies by gender. The average young female spends 71 percent of her activity time on lifetime-oriented activities, but the average young male spends only 56 percent of his time on such activities. Although many physical educators stress the importance of dedicating a major portion of physical education curriculum to lifetime physical activities, the portion of the school physical education curriculum devoted to lifetime fitness in fifth through twelfth grades is only 48 percent—45 percent for boys and 50 percent for girls. *Healthy People 2000* calls for more class time to be spent engaged in lifetime activities and more emphasis to be given to developing the knowledge, attitudes, cognitive skills and physical skills students need to remain physically active throughout life.

In order to achieve these objectives and provide physical education experiences that promote the healthy development of students, the teachers responsible for these programs need inservice education. Prospective teachers need preservice education. District or school level physical education specialists can become responsible for the inservice education of nonspecialized teachers who are responsible for physical education classes. In addition, a team that includes the physical education specialist should assume responsibility for the overall curriculum scope, sequence and implementation.

Worksheet 4 can be used to assess the current physical education program at your school.

School Nutrition and Food Services

The history of school nutrition in America is a study in politics. It wasn't just by chance that the establishment of school lunch programs in the United States coincided with overproduction of food. School lunches became a convenient dumping ground for surplus food commodities, which in turn provided low-cost food for America's children. Surplus farm products (milk, eggs, meat, cheese) were not always the healthiest food.

At the same time, nutrition education emerged as an important function of the U.S. Department of Agriculture, the same organization that had encouraged overproduction of food and established the school lunch assistance programs. In the late 1970s, the U.S. Department of Health and Human Services, after long and difficult negotiations with the Department of Agriculture,

School-Based Physical Education

How established are the following aspects of a physical education program at your school?

Established
Not — Well

All students participate in daily physical education. 1 2 3 4 5 6 7

At least 50 percent of the physical education classroom time is spent
in physical activity. 1 2 3 4 5 6 7

Teachers have curriculum sequentially developed by grade and developmental
level of students. 1 2 3 4 5 6 7

All physical education specialists have teaching certificates in physical education. 1 2 3 4 5 6 7

All classroom teachers responsible for physical education activities of students
have had preservice or inservice physical education preparation. 1 2 3 4 5 6 7

The school physical education program works closely with other community-
based physical activity programs. 1 2 3 4 5 6 7

The activities of the physical education program are closely integrated with
classroom learning in health education. 1 2 3 4 5 6 7

At least 70 percent of the physical education classroom time in upper grades
is devoted to lifetime physical activities. 1 2 3 4 5 6 7

The school physical education program includes schoolwide activities that
promote involvement and participation. 1 2 3 4 5 6 7

Families and community members are routinely involved in school-based
physical education activities. 1 2 3 4 5 6 7

Teachers are trained to adapt physical education programs to meet the
special needs of all students. 1 2 3 4 5 6 7

Teachers and staff have opportunities to participate in school-based
physical activities. 1 2 3 4 5 6 7

Total School-Based Physical Education Score: ____/84

made a series of recommendations in *Dietary Guidelines for Americans*. The 1990 edition of these recommendations urged Americans to

- reduce intake of fat to less than 30 percent and saturated fats to less than 10 percent of the total dietary intake
- increase consumption of fruits and vegetables
- reduce intake of sugar
- increase consumption of whole-grain products
- reduce consumption of salt
- reduce total calorie intake

These guidelines established new criteria for measuring the nutritional value of school lunch programs. Although many schools today incorporate the principles of the *Dietary Guidelines*, such nutritional planning should be universal.

Healthy People 2000 recommends we "increase to at least 90 percent the proportion of school lunch and breakfast services...that are consistent with the nutritional principles in the *Dietary Guidelines for Americans*" (Objective #2.17). To accomplish this objective, school meals must provide choices that include low-fat foods, vegetables, fruits and whole-grain products. Doing so will also provide opportunities for students to practice the health knowledge and food selection skills introduced in school-based health education instruction.

To support this learning experience, *Healthy People 2000* recommends that schools offer "point-of-choice" nutrition information in the school cafeteria. Point-of-choice nutrition information includes information on nutrient value and calories of the foods being served. Such information helps students to choose healthy food.

Healthy People 2000 further recommends that school fundraising activities that involve food sales, onsite vending machine offerings, and food service offerings at concession stands during recreational and other events should reflect the principles of the *Dietary Guidelines for Americans*.

For many children, especially poor children, school breakfast, lunch and snack programs constitute a significant portion of their daily nutritional intake. In these cases, school food service personnel, and particularly cafeteria managers, are the gatekeepers to children's food supply. The school's nutritional program provides an excellent opportunity to establish health norms and model healthy nutritional behaviors. Schools that provide healthy food choices and discourage availability of unhealthy foods send a clear message to developing youth. Schools can also involve students in the planning of menus and preparation of food as a hands-on learning experience.

Nutritional policies consistent with scientific health findings and in the best interests of students demonstrate a school's commitment to the development of healthy youth. Such policies, with opportunities for students to practice nutritional knowledge and food selection skills in the lunch line, are consistent with the overall concept of a healthy school.

The school food services program is an important component of the healthy school. For example, the balance between nutritional intake and exercise is an important factor in proper weight control for students, teachers and staff.

In some communities, school food service personnel spend time in the classroom, working with teachers to deliver nutrition instruction to students and preparing educational materials that enable students' families to support the classroom instruction. For students with special nutritional needs, close cooperation between school health services personnel and food services personnel is a critical factor in these students' achievement of optimal health.

Use Worksheet 5 to evaluate the nutrition and food services at your school.

School-Based Counseling and Personal Support

The school counseling program was originally implemented in the 1960s to provide vocational guidance for students. Today, school counselors and psychologists work in partnership with teachers, parents and community personnel to respond to special needs and provide personal support for individual students, teachers and staff. In addition, in many schools, counseling staff have initiated programs that promote schoolwide mental, emotional and social well-being.

The American School Counselor Association (ASCA) identifies the major aims of school-based counseling as follows:

- to help students increase communication skills

- to improve the quality of interaction between adults and youth

- to encourage the learning process

- to sensitize administrators and teachers to the necessity of matching the curriculum to the developmental needs of the students

The school counselor works to meet these goals by "structuring developmental guidance to promote psychological aspects of human development; individual and small group counseling; consultation with and inservice training for staff, parents and community groups; and performing needs assessment to guide interventions" (Klingman, 1984).

A recent study found that school counselors routinely interact with students on the following issues:

School Nutrition and Food Services

How established are these nutrition and food services at your school?

	Established Not — Well
Inservice nutrition education is routinely provided for food service personnel.	1 2 3 4 5 6 7
The school food service program closely follows the *Dietary Guidelines for Americans*.	1 2 3 4 5 6 7
Point-of-choice nutritional information is routinely provided in the school food program.	1 2 3 4 5 6 7
Food service personnel work closely with health services personnel to meet special needs of students.	1 2 3 4 5 6 7
Fundraising activities involve only healthy food.	1 2 3 4 5 6 7
Students have the opportunity to choose healthy food for school meals.	1 2 3 4 5 6 7
Onsite vending machines offer healthy food.	1 2 3 4 5 6 7
School has written policies regarding nutritional value of food served at school.	1 2 3 4 5 6 7
Food service personnel routinely work with teachers in classroom instruction.	1 2 3 4 5 6 7
Food service personnel routinely work with teachers to understand how they can further the objectives of classroom instruction.	1 2 3 4 5 6 7

Total School Nutrition and Food Services Score: ____/70

- divorce
- substance abuse by students or their parents
- teen sexuality and pregnancy
- depression
- suicide
- sexual and physical abuse
- problems with family members or friends
- concerns about career and future
- questions about the meaning of life

Counselors also often become involved in providing assistance to teachers and other school staff and their families. The activities of school counselors often bring them into contact with families of students and with community health and social service workers. Counselors often become the advocates for students' interests.

Like teachers, counselors must be sensitive to the unique cultural backgrounds of students and their families. An understanding of the family and cultural values that guide students' priorities and decisions is crucial for all who share the responsibility for helping young people grow up healthy. Schools should make special efforts to implement inservice education programs to ensure that counselors have background in and understanding of the communities and cultures in which students live.

Counselors can provide broad-based intervention programs to promote the health of students. They can initiate individual and small group programs aimed at preventing the onset of mental and emotional health problems, as well as interventions designed to reduce the consequences of stress or rehabilitate those who are experiencing difficulty in coping with the stresses of life.

These interventions include:

- problem-solving training
- assertiveness training
- life skills training
- peer-led problem-solving groups
- programs to build self-esteem and address loss of control, peer pressure and adolescent rebellion (Klingman, 1984)

Many schools employ school psychologists. The role of the psychologist varies from school to school. Much of the school psychologist's time is spent on pyscho-educational evaluation and educational programming for students with special needs. In addition, the school psychologist provides:

- group appraisal of students
- coordination with other pupil personnel workers
- coordination with child- and youth-serving community agencies

- counseling and psychotherapy
- preventive mental health consultation
- participation on curriculum committees
- inservice education
- data collection and research

School counselors and psychologists are important members of the school team who contribute to the healthy development of students. Both the counselor and psychologist play an important role in linking schools with families and community health and social service workers and agencies. The resulting partnerships are crucial to creating an environment that supports young people in growing up healthy.

Worksheet 6 allows you to assess your school's current efforts to provide counseling and personal support to students and staff.

Schoolsite Health Promotion

Health promotion is a combination of educational, organizational and environmental activities designed to encourage students and staff to adopt healthier lifestyles and become better consumers of health care services. Like all components in a comprehensive school health program, school-based health promotion is intertwined with and closely linked to the other components.

Health promotion might be viewed as the twine binding the components of a comprehensive school health program together. Health promotion views the school and its activities as a total environment.

School leaders should view health promotion as a systems approach that enables the school to bring together the various health-related components to foster a culture that supports healthy development and the practice of healthy lifestyles. Health promotion establishes a social climate with the following characteristics:

- Teachers and family members are encouraged and enabled to model healthy behaviors.

- Opportunities are provided for students, faculty and staff, and parents and community members to practice health-promoting behaviors.

- Reinforcement is built-in through recognizing and rewarding those who practice healthy behaviors.

- Health services are linked to health instruction.

- Assessment, counseling and, when necessary, referral of students experiencing health-related problems are provided.

- School policies and administrative procedures consistently support the healthy development of youth, teachers and staff.

School-Based Counseling and Personal Support

How established are the following counseling services at your school?

Established
Not — Well

Inservice education focusing on students' culture is routinely provided for school counselors and psychologists. 1 2 3 4 5 6 7

School counselors and psychologists are included on the team that works to create healthy schools. 1 2 3 4 5 6 7

School counselors work closely with the health instruction component, providing support in life skills training for students. 1 2 3 4 5 6 7

Counselors work closely with health services personnel to meet special health needs of students. 1 2 3 4 5 6 7

Counselors and psychologists work closely with families regarding special health needs of students. 1 2 3 4 5 6 7

Counselors and psychologists work closely with community health and social services providers. 1 2 3 4 5 6 7

School has formed a partnership with families and community agencies focusing on the mental/emotional needs of students. 1 2 3 4 5 6 7

Counselors conduct training to help parents and families develop skills that support the healthy development of their children. 1 2 3 4 5 6 7

Counseling personnel routinely work with teachers in health-related classroom instruction. 1 2 3 4 5 6 7

Counseling personnel provide leadership on schoolwide mental and emotional health promotion programs. 1 2 3 4 5 6 7

Counselors and psychologists routinely provide direct services for teachers and school staff. 1 2 3 4 5 6 7

Counselors and psychologists routinely act as advocates for the mental/emotional health of students. 1 2 3 4 5 6 7

Crisis teams deal with overdose, injury or death of student(s) or staff. 1 2 3 4 5 6 7

Peer helper programs provide training and support for peer intervention. 1 2 3 4 5 6 7

Student assistance programs identify, screen and refer students and staff with problems related to alcohol and drug use. 1 2 3 4 5 6 7

Support groups facilitated by trained counselors are provided for students and staff. 1 2 3 4 5 6 7

Counseling Services Score: ____/112

Worksheet 6 continued

How satisfied are you with the school's counseling services in the following areas?

Satisfied
Not — Very

Divorce and family problems 1 2 3 4 5 6 7

Substance use by students... 1 2 3 4 5 6 7

Parents' substance use affecting students.. 1 2 3 4 5 6 7

Teen sexuality 1 2 3 4 5 6 7

Family planning and pregnancy counseling 1 2 3 4 5 6 7

Depression and suicide 1 2 3 4 5 6 7

Students' problems with friends 1 2 3 4 5 6 7

Sexual and physical abuse.. 1 2 3 4 5 6 7

Career counseling... 1 2 3 4 5 6 7

Academic counseling 1 2 3 4 5 6 7

Youth employment.. 1 2 3 4 5 6 7

Counseling Satisfaction Score: ____/77

Worksheet 6 continued

How prepared are your counselors to provide support to students in the following areas?

	Prepared *Not — Well*
Divorce and family problems	1 2 3 4 5 6 7
Substance use by students	1 2 3 4 5 6 7
Parents' substance use affecting students	1 2 3 4 5 6 7
Teen sexuality	1 2 3 4 5 6 7
Family planning and pregnancy counseling	1 2 3 4 5 6 7
Depression and suicide	1 2 3 4 5 6 7
Students' problems with friends	1 2 3 4 5 6 7
Sexual and physical abuse	1 2 3 4 5 6 7
Career counseling	1 2 3 4 5 6 7
Academic counseling	1 2 3 4 5 6 7
Youth employment	1 2 3 4 5 6 7

Counselors' Preparation Score: ____/77

What best describes your school counseling efforts to support students' development of health-related skills in the following areas?

	Developed *Not — Highly*
Programs to build self-esteem	1 2 3 4 5 6 7
Programs to help students address loss of control	1 2 3 4 5 6 7
Programs to help students resist peer pressure	1 2 3 4 5 6 7
Programs to help students develop problem-solving skills	1 2 3 4 5 6 7
Programs addressing adolescent issues	1 2 3 4 5 6 7
Programs to help students develop assertiveness skills	1 2 3 4 5 6 7

Counseling Programs Score: ____/42

Total School-Based Counseling and Personal Support Score: ____/308

The documented effects of health promotion programs on staff include increased energy levels, increased productivity, improved morale, decreased absenteeism and decreased teacher burnout.

Teachers and school staff who model the health knowledge, skills and behaviors taught in the classroom encourage students to adopt healthy behaviors. School policies and practices that provide a health-promoting environment free from violence and pressures to engage in self-destructive health behaviors provide an opportunity for students to adopt healthy behaviors.

Providing for the safety of students is only the first step in establishing a health-promoting environment in the school. Schools can provide other health-promoting opportunities as well. These include:

- opportunities to select food in the school cafeteria that is low in fat, high in nutrients and prepared in a healthy manner

- a smoke-free environment in which to learn

- opportunities for all students to engage in physical activities that promote cardiovascular fitness, flexibility, strength and coordination and that can be practiced over the life span

Social values and cultural beliefs and traditions are important determinants of health behavior. The school must reach beyond the schoolyard gate and work with families and communities to understand the social and cultural aspects of health. Then it can help communities and families develop culturally specific programs that provide health-promoting activities that reinforce those of the school.

The health and social norms of the home and community support or detract from a school's ability to foster the development of healthy youth. Communities that value healthy behaviors can send a clear message supporting young people's adoption of healthy behaviors. The following activities can be part of that message:

- modeling healthy behavior

- providing environmental support (such as enforcement of laws against the sale of alcohol to minors)

- having health care providers inquire about and offer counsel regarding healthy behaviors

- providing opportunities for young and old alike to practice health-promoting behavior

The school's role in establishing the health-promotion component includes:

- appointment of a leader

- formation of a school and community health council

- work with the community and families

to conceive and articulate a vision for the healthy development of children

- analysis of the current school, community and family environment for health promotion and support of the healthy development of students

- development and implementation of new policies, programs and strategies that fully utilize the resources of the school, community and families to help children grow up healthy

To achieve ultimate effectiveness, school-site health promotion should involve the following people:

- board of education members as policy makers to provide overall direction

- districtwide and school-based administrators as program enablers and supporters

- program leaders, including school-based personnel, health and social service professionals, community members and parents, responsible for identifying needs, and developing and implementing programs. (In addition to the identified health-promotion leader, school-based personnel includes all teachers; counselors and psychological staff; school nurses, physicians, dentists and others providing health services; health education specialists, dietitians and

food service personnel; and physical education specialists.)

- students, teachers and staff, and community and family members as participants and recipients of the health promotion programs

As with all programs, education and training will enhance the success of the school health-promotion program. In more than one-half of the states, department of education and department of health leaders offer five-day statewide summer wellness conferences for school teams comprised of administrators, teachers, staff and community leaders.

These teams learn how to incorporate the concept of "wellness as a lifestyle" into their personal and professional lives. When these teams return to their home communities, they have the knowledge, skills and commitment to establish health-promotion efforts in their schools and communities.

The specific types of education and training necessary to establish school-based health promotion programs include:

- Teacher education to help teachers understand the relationship between health and education, the importance and techniques of forming partnerships with families and communities, the cultural and traditional beliefs of the community, specific health knowledge and health skills development, integration of health education into the existing course offerings, and the importance and techniques of modeling healthy behaviors.

- Education for principals, food service, building maintenance, security, health care and other staff to help them identify their roles in the overall efforts to develop a health-promoting environment within the school.

- Family education that involves parents in the ongoing health education curriculum and provides them with knowledge and skills that will enable them to supplement and support the classroom instruction and provide opportunities for practice and reinforcement for their children's healthy behaviors at home.

- Education that enables community members and organizations to assume their responsibilities for fostering the development of policy, programs and activities that promote healthy development of children and youth.

- Advocacy training that enables all school personnel, health and social service professionals, and community and family members to organize to support the healthy development of young people.

Worksheet 7 allows you to assess your school's current schoolsite health promotion efforts.

School, Family and Community Health Promotion Partnerships

Smoking, alcohol and other drug use, sexual activity at an early age, violence and abuse, delinquency and school drop-out are not school problems. These interrelated threats to the future health of youth share common roots in the community, families and school.

Partnerships to unite schools, families and communities are being established across America to help solve these communitywide problems. These effective collaborative partnerships focus on health promotion and disease prevention. Collaborative efforts are the cornerstone of prevention and the foundation upon which children develop to their fullest potential. School officials have a leadership role to play in these efforts.

Schools and communities cannot ignore the role poverty plays in limiting children's access to health and education and subsequently, opportunities for success in the twenty-first century. Appropriate health education for poor children and children of diverse ethnic backgrounds should be devised in consultation with those who represent their culture.

Schoolsite Health Promotion

What priority does your school give to these health promotion activities?

Priority
Low — High

Fully utilizing school facilities to promote health 1 2 3 4 5 6 7

Providing healthy food choices for teachers and staff in the school cafeteria 1 2 3 4 5 6 7

Providing a smoke-free environment 1 2 3 4 5 6 7

Providing an environment free of alcohol and other drugs 1 2 3 4 5 6 7

Sponsoring smoking cessation classes 1 2 3 4 5 6 7

Sponsoring exercise and fitness classes 1 2 3 4 5 6 7

Sponsoring weight control classes 1 2 3 4 5 6 7

Providing routine health screenings (e.g., blood pressure, cholesterol) for staff 1 2 3 4 5 6 7

Providing employee assistance programs for screening, referral, counseling and
rehabilitation for staff 1 2 3 4 5 6 7

Offering self-improvement classes 1 2 3 4 5 6 7

Working with communities to ensure existence of policies and laws that support
healthy behavior 1 2 3 4 5 6 7

Stressing a prevention focus for school health and counseling and
psychological services 1 2 3 4 5 6 7

Sponsoring education that enables school personnel to develop a health-promoting
environment 1 2 3 4 5 6 7

Having teachers who are healthy physical, social and emotional role models 1 2 3 4 5 6 7

Working with families to increase their ability to provide opportunities to practice
and reinforce healthy behaviors 1 2 3 4 5 6 7

Total Schoolsite Health Promotion Score: _____/105

Partnerships formed to support the healthy development of children must involve parents from all cultures and business and community leaders representing the ethnic as well as the economic diversity of the community. It is particularly critical to involve parents who are members of poor communities. To ignore this area will result in social and educational failure for thousands of young people. For many, this failure will be will be the precursor of an adult life of poor health, crime, unemployment, welfare dependency and premature death. This is an unacceptable vision for our children. Coalitions and partnerships driven by mutual aspirations that share a common vision of healthy young people can effectively help schools meet the needs of youth.

Code Blue: Uniting for Healthier Youth— A Call to Action, a report of the National Commission on the Role of the School and Community in Improving Adolescent Health (1990), issued a call for national action to improve the health of youth. The commission was jointly convened by the National Association of State Boards of Education and the American Medical Association. The report identified all sectors of society as important actors, including:

- individual Americans
- federal and state governments
- local communities
- health and social services communities
- businesses and corporations
- media, entertainment and advertising industries
- churches, youth-serving agencies and other community organizations
- the education community

Recommendations for collaborative action were directed to each of these sectors. Among those recommendations aimed at the education community were the following:

- Education and health are inextricably intertwined. Achieving the educational mission requires attending to the health needs of students.

- Recognize the necessity of working with not only students, but their families, whatever the composition of such families might be.

- Promote the concept of collaboration within the school and welcome other health professional and service delivery organizations to the school as full partners in working with students.

- Permit sharing of information with collaborating agencies on a need-to-know basis that maintains confidentiality.

- Allow schools to serve as locations for student health care if the local community determines that school sites are the most effective location for providing collaborative services.

- Make school buildings available as sites for recreation, services and other community activities outside school hours.

- Provide all students opportunities to engage in community service.

The commission concluded its recommendations to the educational community by urging education leaders to ensure that teachers are trained in collaborative approaches and given sufficient time to work with other professionals, community members and families.

Collaboration with families requires that schools engage families in the education of their children. This can be done by giving families meaningful roles in school governance, communicating with families about the school program and student progress, and offering families opportunities to support the learning process at home and at school (Carnegie Council on Adolescent Development, 1989). For example, homework assignments that draw on the family's history and experiences or views regarding current health affairs help engage youth and their families with the school.

Worksheet 8 allows you to evaluate your school's current efforts to establish collaborative partnerships with communities and families to support the healthy growth and development of your students.

School, Family and Community Health Promotion Efforts

What describes your school's current efforts on the following activities to promote partnerships for healthy development of your students?

The school participates in a health coalition with community members, health and social agencies and parents. 1 2 3 4 5 6 7

The school shares information with collaborating community agencies. 1 2 3 4 5 6 7

Partnerships include representation from a variety of cultures and income levels. 1 2 3 4 5 6 7

The school serves as a center of community activities during non-school hours. 1 2 3 4 5 6 7

Students have an opportunity to engage in community service. 1 2 3 4 5 6 7

Teachers are educated in working in collaboration with community and family members. 1 2 3 4 5 6 7

Teachers are provided sufficient time to work in collaboration with professionals and community and family members. 1 2 3 4 5 6 7

Teachers routinely visit the families and homes of students. 1 2 3 4 5 6 7

Teachers routinely assign health-related learning activities that involve students' families. 1 2 3 4 5 6 7

School and teachers routinely work with health and social service professionals. 1 2 3 4 5 6 7

The school routinely negotiates students' health needs with health care providers.....1 2 3 4 5 6 7

Health workers are routinely involved in school and classroom teaching and learning activities. 1 2 3 4 5 6 7

Parent education programs on health topics are routinely offered. 1 2 3 4 5 6 7

Family and community members have a voice in the school's health education programs. 1 2 3 4 5 6 7

The school shares mutual aspirations and visions for students with families and the community. 1 2 3 4 5 6 7

Money is routinely budgeted for collaboration with community organizations. 1 2 3 4 5 6 7

Clear and mutual goals for the health of students have been agreed on by the school, families and the community. 1 2 3 4 5 6 7

Group meetings between the school and community are frequent and ongoing. 1 2 3 4 5 6 7

Staff person is assigned the responsibility for creating partnerships focusing on healthy youth. 1 2 3 4 5 6 7

The school shares a sense of ownership with families and communities regarding the healthy vision for youth. 1 2 3 4 5 6 7

Total School, Family and Community Health Promotion Score: ____/140

3

Developing a Comprehensive School Health Program

This section is designed to answer the question of how school leaders go about establishing a comprehensive school health program. The following step-by-step approach walks you through the development of such a program. The steps include:

- needs assessment
- organization of support and working groups
- goal development
- program status assessment
- resource analysis
- development and implementation of a strategic plan
- evaluation
- a process for monitoring and managing change

STEP 1

Establish an Ad Hoc Advisory Committee

The establishment of an ad hoc advisory committee is the first step in developing the program. This group acts as a "cabinet" to assist and advise school leaders in their efforts to initiate the planning for the school's comprehensive school health program. The ad hoc advisory committee advises school leaders during the initial stages of planning; it is discontinued once the Committee for Healthy Students is established. Members of the ad hoc committee should be selected based on the following criteria:

- the school's need for health expertise
- their access to ongoing community initiatives

- their vision of health and education challenges
- their knowledge of and access to school and community organizations
- their visibility and established leadership qualities

The nature of this committee's responsibilities suggests it should have five to eight members. Ideally, membership should include:

- a school board member
- a local or state epidemiologist
- community leaders (church, social, organizational, political)
- community health and social service personnel
- teachers and other school leaders

The functions of the committee are as follows:

- Reviews and clarifies the need for a vision of a comprehensive school program that supports healthy development of children.
- Identifies strategies and opportunities for schools, families and communities to come together to develop this vision.
- Advises school leaders on assessing community aspirations.

- Assists school leaders with the epidemiological assessment of the health status of children in the community.
- Advises school leaders regarding the establishment and membership of a Committee for Healthy Students.

Follow these steps to establish the Ad Hoc Advisory Committee:

1. Review the gaps in your current knowledge and expertise, and identify steps, individuals and resources needed to bring schools, families and the community together.

2. Review and evaluate existing membership of groups with similar interests.

3. Identify key individuals in the community who could represent the knowledge and expertise the school needs.

4. Contact potential members by telephone. Describe your request and indicate you will follow up with a letter requesting them to serve.

5. Send the follow-up letter. It should include:

   - a statement of the need
   - overall charge of the committee
   - specific responsibilities members are asked to assume
   - an estimate of the time commitment and length of service required
   - a date for the first meeting

6. Host the first meeting.

    *   Send agenda, list of participants, starting and ending times, background information and contact person for more information one week prior to the meeting.

    *   Describe the need and discuss the importance of establishing a vision.

    *   Discuss role, function and expected products and timeline for committee activities.

    *   Establish operating procedures.

    *   Select a chairperson.

    *   Clarify work and responsibilities to be completed by the next meeting.

    *   Establish date and tentative agenda for the next meeting.

STEP 2

Assess Community Aspirations

The community's aspirations and perceptions of health needs must be identified. Sources of this information include:

*   students

*   parents and family members

*   church leaders

*   community leaders

*   health and social services professionals

*   teachers and other school personnel

*   supportive community members*

Community aspirations and values, when described, should provide philosophical foundation for establishing the school's comprehensive school health program. Consulting with the community regarding their concerns not only provides valuable input that can guide program development, but is also an important first step in establishing community ownership of the program.

Because each community is different, school leaders will have to determine the most effective methods of working with their community to collect information. Issues related to reading levels, written and spoken language proficiency, cultural differences and access to decision making need to be considered in this process. School leaders should collect information from all segments of the community to ensure a clear understanding of the community's concerns. Suggested approaches include:

*   formal meetings that utilize consensus approaches, such as nominal group process

*   informal meetings and discussions

---

* These are people without children in the schools, but with high aspirations for children's health, welfare and happiness.

- questionnaires mailed to community members
- questionnaires as follow-ups to meetings
- questionnaires at drop-in centers or community functions
- telephone surveys
- personal interviews

School leaders can either create opportunities for securing community input or take advantage of existing mechanisms. Data collection mechanisms include:

- town hall meetings
- meetings with specific identified groups (church, social, professional, civic)
- a special telephone line established to encourage input
- radio talk shows with call-in responses
- staffed booths at malls, community centers and public events
- consultation with community leaders

Figures 6 and 7 provide sample questionnaires that can be used to gather information.

STEP 3

Use Epidemiologic Data to Identify Student Needs

Identifying, assembling and interpreting epidemiologic data can best be carried out by public health personnel who have a background in and understanding of epidemiology. Including a public health epidemiologist on the ad hoc committee helps ensure that the school's programs consider the latest health and risk-factor data pertinent to school-age children and youth. The following suggestions can help the school administrator articulate the type of data needed and the possible uses of that data in developing school health programs.

Mortality data for school-age children and youth should have the following characteristics:

- Presented for the most localized unit possible (school, community/town, county, state or national). Most areas will have mortality data available by county. Some will have data available for cities and even areas within the city.
- Displayed by cause of death with rates to allow comparisons.
- Displayed by age group.
- Displayed by gender.

Figure 6

Questions for Parents, Families and Community Members

1. What is one wish that you have for your children (or the children of our community)?

   _____

2. What three things about your life give you the greatest happiness?

   _____

   _____

   _____

3. What are the three biggest barriers to your attempts to achieve personal happiness?

   _____

   _____

   _____

4. What worries you most about your children and the lives they currently live?

   _____

   _____

   _____

5. What worries do you have about your children's health and safety?

   a. Currently _____

   b. In the next five years _____

   c. In the next ten years _____

   d. In the next twenty years _____

   e. Beyond the next twenty years _____

Figure 6 continued

6. If you could do anything, what would you do to ensure the happiness of our community's children?_____

_____

_____

_____

7. What could the schools do to make this community healthier and safer?

_____

_____

_____

_____

_____

_____

8. What could the community do to make children's lives healthier and safer?

_____

_____

_____

_____

9. What three suggestions do you have for the schools to ensure that our children grow up healthy and reach their fullest potential?

_____

_____

_____

_____

_____

_____

Figure 7

Questions for Students

1. What three things in your life give you your greatest happiness?

_____

_____

_____

2. What three things do you worry about most?

_____

_____

_____

3. If you could change one thing to make you happier, what would it be?

_____

_____

_____

_____

_____

_____

_____

_____

_____

4. Rate your current level of health:

	Very Unhealthy			Average Health			Very Healthy		
Physical Health	1	2	3	4	5	6	7	8	9
Mental/Emotional Health	1	2	3	4	5	6	7	8	9

Figure 7 continued

5. How healthy do you expect to be at the following ages?

	Very Unhealthy			Average Health			Very Healthy		
age 25	1	2	3	4	5	6	7	8	9
age 45	1	2	3	4	5	6	7	8	9
age 65	1	2	3	4	5	6	7	8	9
age 85	1	2	3	4	5	6	7	8	9

6. What two things could the school do to make your life healthier and safer?

_____

_____

7. What two things could the community do to make your life healthier and safer?

_____

_____

8. What two things could your family do to make your life healthier and safer?

_____

_____

9. How can this school help your family achieve happier and healthier lives?

_____

_____

_____

_____

_____

In some cases, grouping data by race or ethnicity may be useful; however "victim blaming" often results from reporting data in this matter and can be counterproductive. (For example, blaming young African-American men for being frequent victims of homicide does nothing to stop premature death.) School leaders should be particularly interested in deaths from causes with known risk factors and effective educational interventions.

Morbidity (injury and sickness) data for school-age children should also be considered, keeping in mind the following points:

- Morbidity data is far less reliable and less standardized than mortality data. School leaders may find that data exists for some areas and not for others.

- Morbidity data may include hospital admissions and days missed from school for specific causes or number of cases of sexually transmitted and other reportable diseases.

- Data regarding teenage pregnancies, although not fitting the classic definition of morbidity, is important health status data for schools to consider.

- Health services data, including immunization status, prenatal care for teenage mothers, mental health consultations, and alcohol and drug treatment referrals among youth, can help school leaders get a fuller picture of the health of the community's children.

Behavioral risk-factor data quantifies the presence of risky or health protective behaviors in a population. Identifying behavior risk factors among school-age youth is an important step in developing educational and preventive interventions. Most risk-factor data is reported as the incidence and/or prevalence of negative health behaviors. Typical risk factor information will include the incidence, prevalence and age at onset of:

- tobacco use
- alcohol and drug use
- sexual intercourse
- unprotected sexual intercourse
- nonuse of safety belts
- engagement in violence
- levels of nonexercise
- obesity
- quantity of unhealthy food consumed

School leaders should attempt to develop an epidemiologic report that clearly outlines the health status, access to health services and risk factors of the community's children and youth that can be understood by the average fifth to seventh grade student.

Convene an Awareness Meeting of Students, Parents and Community Members

Once school leaders have completed and digested the community needs assessment and the epidemiologic assessment of the health status of children and youth, an open forum should be held. The open forum serves several purposes:

- It demonstrates to those community members who provided input that school leaders were listening to their ideas and concerns.

- It provides an opportunity to build on the ideas and concerns of community members by presenting epidemiologic data regarding health status of children and youth.

- It provides a first opportunity for school leaders to present the community concerns and epidemiologic information to the other community leaders and the press.

- It provides an opportunity to begin to develop a cadre of community leaders who will be asked to commit time and energy to the idea of schools taking a leadership role in the devel-

opment of healthy children and youth. These individuals will be asked to serve on committees and provide support for the overall efforts.

- It provides an opportunity for children and youth to begin to grasp the concerns, expectations and support community leaders have for their healthy development.

The meeting should be planned well in advance and given high visibility. A joint school and community (city, organizations, agencies) sponsorship will help ensure the level of commitment and visibility desired. In order to accommodate the wide range of needs that exist in most communities, school leaders should keep in mind the following points:

- The major themes and key points of information should be available in an easy to read (fifth to seventh grade reading level) handout for all attendees. The information should be modified to meet the needs of the community's major non-English-reading populations.

- Presentations should be accompanied with clear graphs and charts visible to all attendees and duplicated (if possible) in a handout for those who desire the information (particularly press representatives).

- The forum should be at an opportune time (beginning of the school year, summer break), which could mark the beginning of a new program. It should also be at a time when working parents can attend.

STEP 5

Establish the Committee for Healthy Students

The Committee for Healthy Students is responsible for securing broad-based community support and input for the comprehensive school health program. The committee acts as an advisory and steering committee, providing the overall direction for the program.

The membership of the Committee for Healthy Students needs to be broad enough to represent the various organizations and agencies with an interest in the healthy development of youth. Every attempt should be made to include individuals who can represent an organization's unique perspective, but can forego the organization's individual agenda in favor of the broad agenda of establishing a systematic and comprehensive school health program. It is also important to include parents and other community members who are not affiliated with a particular group. Worksheet 9 presents a check-

list to help school leaders select committee members.

The Committee for Healthy Students has the following functions:

- Demonstrates official organizational commitment to a comprehensive approach to ensure optional student health.

- Contributes unique organizational perspective, resources and materials to the overall goal.

- Develops and refines a shared vision for the school's role in developing healthy children and youth.

- Carries information back to membership of constituent organizations.

- Provides concrete direction for implementing a school program based on the shared vision.

- Reviews recommendations of working groups, develops the five-year strategic plan, and makes recommendations to the board of education regarding program focus, priorities, timelines and budgets.

- Periodically reviews evaluation data and suggests program changes and priorities.

Follow these steps to establish the Committee for Healthy Students:

1. Review requirements for representation

Committee for Healthy Students
Potential Members

Organization	Phone #	Has Health Education Program		Contact Person
		Yes	No	
Community-Based Organizations		☐	☐	
		☐	☐	
Parent Organizations		☐	☐	
		☐	☐	
Youth Serving Organizations		☐	☐	
		☐	☐	
Voluntary Health Organizations		☐	☐	
		☐	☐	
Social Organizations		☐	☐	
		☐	☐	
Private Businesses/Industry		☐	☐	
		☐	☐	
Health Care Providers		☐	☐	
		☐	☐	
Health Care Facilities		☐	☐	
		☐	☐	
Community Support Groups		☐	☐	
		☐	☐	
Churches		☐	☐	
		☐	☐	
Institutions of Higher Education		☐	☐	
		☐	☐	
Law Enforcement Agencies		☐	☐	
		☐	☐	

from community groups and agencies, students and school officials. Identify qualities of potential members, such as access to power and ability to bring school and community together.

2. Review and evaluate existing membership of groups with special interest in the health of children and youth.

3. Identify key individuals in the community who could represent the passion, knowledge and expertise needed to develop programs for children and youth.

4. Develop a one-page synopsis of the need for establishing a comprehensive program to foster healthy development of children and youth.

5. Contact potential members by telephone or in person. Describe your request and indicate you will follow up with a letter requesting them to serve.

6. Send the follow-up letter. It should include:

   • a statement of the need

   • overall charge of the Committee for Healthy Students

   • specific responsibilities members are asked to assume

   • an estimate of the time commitment and length of service required

   • a date for the first meeting

7. Host the first meeting.

   • Send agenda, list of participants, starting and ending times, background information and contact person for more information one week prior to the meeting.

   • Describe the need for and processes for establishing a vision statement.

   • Discuss role, function and expected products and timeline for committee and working group activities.

   • Discuss the importance of continuity of service on the committee and working groups.

   • Establish operating procedures.

   • Select a chairperson.

   • Select leaders of working groups.

   • Clarify work and responsibilities to be completed by the next meeting.

   • Establish date and tentative agenda for the next meeting.

STEP 6

Develop a Shared Vision

An important early step to ensure success of your community's efforts to provide a school program that promotes the development of healthy youth is to develop a vision for the program. Students, parents, community leaders and school personnel should all contribute to the development of this vision statement.

The process of a community contemplating, discussing, drafting, negotiating and coming to consensus on a vision of healthy children and youth helps ensure understanding and support for your school's effort. Those who do not share the experience of developing the community's vision will have more difficulty supporting your efforts. Once developed, the vision statement needs to have high visibility in the community and in all activities related to the school's program.

There are three types of information that the Committee for Healthy Students needs to consider in the process of developing a vision statement: the community's aspirations for and perceptions of the health needs of its children and youth; epidemiological data about the health status and risk behaviors of children and youth; and information regarding proven methods for helping children and youth develop in healthy ways. The following steps will help school leaders organize and facilitate the development of a vision statement.

1. Develop a series of one-page summaries which clearly and briefly state the aspirations and perceptions of health needs as identified by:

    - students

    - parents and family members

    - community members and church leaders

    - health, social service and school personnel

2. Develop a one-page summary of the current health status of children and youth; the risky behaviors in which they currently engage; and family, school and community patterns which contribute to poor health status and increased risks for children and youth.

3. Develop a three-page summary of methods that work to develop healthy children and youth. This should include a synopsis of health education and promotion; behavioral and educational theory and research; school, family and community characteristics which support healthy development; and results of school-based health education evaluations.

4. Host a discussion in which committee members have an opportunity to ask questions about and comment on these summary reports. Assist the committee in their efforts to work through each report. Committee members will be able to help each other clarify the aspirations and perceived needs. It will be important, however, to have an expert health spokesperson lead the discussion and help

the committee understand the epi-demiologic information, and an expert (health educator, behavioral scientist, educational specialist) to help the committee understand the theory, research and evaluation information.

5. Break the committee into small groups (three to five people each). Instruct each group to appoint a recorder and a spokes-person who will be responsible for reporting back to the larger group. Instruct each group to begin to form-ulate a vision statement using the following steps:

   • Identify five words which best describe our aspirations for the health of children and youth.

   • Develop three sentences which capture the community's aspirations for the health of children and youth.

   • Develop three sentences which describe the role of schools, families and communities in helping children and youth grow up healthy.

   Allow approximately twenty minutes for the groups to develop these ideas.

6. Provide ten minutes for each group to present its work to the other committee members. An effective strategy is for the spokesperson to present first and then allow other small group members to clarify and expand on the presentation. Provide a staff person who will record the major points of the presentation in a manner which will allow all participants to review them later.

7. In the large group, the facilitator should summarize and work toward consensus on the major points presented by the small groups. This can be done by bring-ing similar points made by the small groups into a series of statements which articulate a vision. One effective strategy is to identify key words which describe the vision. It will be necessary for the group facilitator to seek consensus on the major points and key words from all participants prior to the conclusion of the activity.

8. School leaders will need time to work with the major points and key words to draft a vision statement. Committee members should be informed that they will receive a draft vision statement for review within ten days following the meeting.

9. School leaders should formulate a draft vision statement or statements (some may prefer to develop two or three similar drafts) then mail the statement(s) to committee members for review, comment or suggested modifications.

10. Once consensus is achieved on a vision statement, the statement should be

brought back to the next meeting of the Committee for Healthy Students for discussion and endorsement.

11. Once accepted by the committee, the vision statement should receive wide distribution and publicity and become the basis upon which all future plans for health education programs are built.

STEP 7

Establish Working Groups

Ideally, school leaders will want to establish one working group for each of the eight areas described in Section 2:

- school health education (instruction)
- healthy school environment
- school health services
- school-based physical education
- school nutrition and food services
- school-based counseling and personal support
- schoolsite health promotion
- school, family and community health promotion partnerships

Small districts may have to combine areas based on the number of people involved. The working groups will support the school's efforts in each area. Each working group will need a coordinator to facilitate the group's activities.

The functions of the working groups are as follows:

- Develop statements that describe the relationship of each school health component to the overall vision shared by families, school personnel and community members.

- Develop goals and objectives that describe the desired outcomes for each component.

- Describe the policies, programs, resources, activities and staffing necessary for each component to make its most useful contribution to the overall goal of healthy children and youth.

- Assess the degree to which programs, resources, activities and necessary staffing are already in place.

- Develop a list of needs (programs, policies, resources, activities, staff) for each component.

- Prioritize the list of needs.

- Assess and develop a list of current resources available to help meet the program needs.

- Identify model curricula and programs available for use in the school.

- Make recommendations regarding a timeline for developing needed policies, programs, resources, activities and hiring or preparing staff.

Follow these steps to establish the working groups:

1. Develop a one-page draft which summarizes the charge of each working group and the relationship of each group's work to the vision and overall plan.

2. Identify members of the Committee for Healthy Students who will be asked to coordinate each working group.

3. Identify a key staff person responsible for facilitating the work of each working group. This person will work directly with the working group coordinator and serve as a liaison to other working groups and school leaders.

4. Identify and invite school staff and faculty with interest and expertise to serve on the appropriate working groups.

5. Hold a planning meeting of the coordinators, key staff people, and selected faculty and staff to discuss potential membership of working groups.

   - Review and evaluate existing membership of the Committee for Healthy Students for potential members for each working group.

   - Identify key individuals in the community who have knowledge and expertise related to the area of each working group.

   - Review the overall charge for the working groups. Develop a charge for each of the eight working groups which includes the responsibilities and length of service being requested of members.

6. Following the meeting contact potential members by telephone or in person. Describe your request and indicate you will follow up with a letter requesting them to serve on the working group.

7. Send the follow-up letter. It should include:

   - a statement of the vision

   - a one-paragraph synopsis describing the relation of the working group and the component they are to develop to other components and the overall plan and vision

   - the charge to the working group including the specific responsibilities of working group members

   - an estimate of the time commitment and length of service required

   - a date and assignments (if any) for the first meeting

STEP 8

Assess the School's Current Program Status

Assessing existing programs and the current status of efforts to promote the health of children and youth is the critical next step. Each working group coordinator should be charged with getting the group to seek answers to the following questions:

- What should be the goals of this component of the school program?

- What policies, programs and resources are currently in place to promote the development of healthy children and youth?

- To what extent is this component currently functioning?

- What more is needed in this area to promote the development of healthy children and youth?

- What model programs currently exist from publishers or other school districts?

In exploring the status of current programs that promote the development of healthy children and youth, working groups need to consider not only schoolsite policies and programs, but programs within the community (youth groups, churches, agencies) that may or may not be currently linked to the schools. The term *programs* is used in the broadest sense. Working groups will want to assess the current status of the full range of activities designed to support development of healthy children and youth. These include:

- policies

- regulations

- services

- educational and learning activities

- opportunities to practice healthy behaviors

- support provided for students who practice healthy behaviors

- role models available in school, at home and in the community

- resources

The worksheets provided in Section 2 will be useful tools for working groups attempting to assess the current status of the eight components. The report from each working group to the Committee for Healthy Students should begin with a description of the proposed goals and the current status of elements and activities within the component that support the healthy development of children and youth.

STEP 9

Identify New Program Needs

The identification of new program needs will result from the assessments carried out by each working group. Working groups should be asked to identify two types of needs: (1) the need for new programs, policies, resources, services and activities to contribute to the overall vision of healthy children and youth, and (2) the areas where existing programs, policies, resources, services and activities need to be strengthen or modified to contribute more effectively to the overall vision.

After compiling a list of needs, each working group must prioritize the needs in terms of their importance and the feasibility of developing programs that effectively meet the need. In prioritizing, working group members must also consider the level of work involved and the amount of money and time required to develop and implement activities to meet each need. The following issues should be considered by working groups as they attempt to prioritize the needs:

- Potential magnitude or effects of the proposed action, including the number of students positively affected, the degree of effect in terms of health behavior and the potential for the program to make a difference.

- The potency of the strategy (policy, regulation, skills development, behavior change) by which the action will be carried out.

- Workload and staff time required to develop and implement the action.

- The cost or loss incurred if the action is delayed or not taken.

- The costs associated with taking the action. Cost will include actual dollar costs of development and implementation as well as "opportunities forgone" (i.e., opportunities missed because the decision to invest time and energy in one action precluded spending time and money on other possible actions).

- Resources (staff, knowledge and expertise, materials, equipment) currently available to develop and implement the program versus new resources needed.

- Readiness of the school and community to embrace the action. For example, research shows that sexuality education combined with skills training and the availability of contraceptives is effective in reducing unwanted teen pregnancies. But school leaders may find some communities are not yet ready for such a three-tiered approach to reducing teen pregnancies.

- Administrative ease in developing and implementing the action.

- Community awareness regarding program needs and staff inservice training necessary for school personnel to implement the program.

Working committees can use Worksheet 10 to help them prioritize the needs.

STEP 10

Develop Program Goals and Objectives for Each Area

Program goals are general statements that attempt to describe the desired outcome, thus providing a clear picture of program intent. Program goals provide direction for decisions regarding specific outcomes, activities and services, materials, staff, and evaluation models to monitor the program. Specific program objectives that allow for measurement of progress should also be established. Careful monitoring and evaluation of program objectives will allow school leaders to make decisions regarding allocation of program resources, implementation of new approaches and discontinuation of activities.

Once the needs in each component have been identified, working groups should develop program goals and objectives for each component. The following steps are suggested to facilitate program goal and objective development:

1. Write one or more general statements (program goals) that reflect the school's intent to develop this component to support the overall vision of healthy children. For example, the long range goal for the school food service component might be "to provide healthy lunches and snacks for students."

2. For each program goal, develop specific, measurable program objectives based on the results of the assessment of the eight components of the school health program. (See Worksheet 11.) These program objectives can describe the intent to continue existing activities as well as develop new activities to meet identified needs. Program objectives can be related to provision of services, staffing, educational activities, policies and administrative rules, collaboration with families and community or any other activities that help the school meet the program goal.

Program objectives should include a description of what is to be accomplished and who the audience is. For example, Worksheet 12 shows two program objectives related to the program goal, "to

Priority of Needs for Programs, Services, Policies and Activities

Criterion	*Needs*		
	1. _____	2. _____	3. _____
number of students affected	_____	_____	_____
magnitude of the problem or issue (on a scale of 1 to 10)	_____	_____	_____
readiness of the school (1–10)	_____	_____	_____
readiness of the community (1–10)	_____	_____	_____
potency of strategy (1–10)	_____	_____	_____
administrative ease (1–10)	_____	_____	_____
workload required (1–10)	_____	_____	_____
level of community awareness necessary (1–10)	_____	_____	_____
level of inservice training necessary (1–10)	_____	_____	_____
resources available (1–10)	_____	_____	_____
costs of action	_____	_____	_____
costs of inaction	_____	_____	_____
time until completion	_____	_____	_____

provide healthy lunches and snacks for students." These two objectives are that "All meals provided by the school cafeteria to students and staff will contain less than 25 percent of calories from fats" and "All schools will serve only juices and water (no soda pop) in drink vending machines."

STEP 11

Conduct Resources Assessment

Once each working group has identified and prioritized its component's needs, an assessment of school and community resources available to help meet these needs should be conducted. Only those needs identified as highest priority should be considered. Working group members will want to explore all available resources, including resources of the school, students and families, and community members and groups available to support program development.

Resources to be considered include:

- policies currently in place to support the proposed actions
- staff and community workers available
- level of expertise or readiness of teachers and school staff
- curriculum, teaching/learning materials, textbooks and supplies

- equipment and facilities (e.g., track, gymnasium, health center)
- community resources (e.g., counselors, self-help groups)

STEP 12

Working Groups Present Reports to the Committee for Healthy Students

Each working group coordinator will be responsible for delivering the group's report to the Committee for Healthy Students. Reports from each of the working group coordinators should be presented at a meeting of the committee. Working group reports should include:

- statement of the importance of the component examined by the working group to the overall development of healthy children and youth
- prioritized goals with objectives, activities, timelines, staffing and evaluations
- resources available to implement the activities
- special issues or problems
- recommendations

Program Goals and Objectives

Program Goal

_____

_____

_____

Program Objectives

1. _____

_____

_____

2. _____

_____

_____

3. _____

_____

_____

4. _____

_____

_____

5. _____

_____

_____

Sample Program Goal and Objectives

Program Goal

To provide healthy lunches and snacks for students

Program Objectives

1. All meals provided by the school cafeteria to students and staff will contain less than 25 percent of calories from fats.

2. All schools will serve only juices and water (no soda pop) in drink vending machines.

The Committee for Healthy Students has the responsibility of developing the strategic plan and presenting the final recommendations to the school leaders and local board of education for action. The reports from each working group can serve as the basis for the committee's strategic plan.

Step 13

Committee for Healthy Students Develops the Strategic Plan

The Committee for Healthy Students is responsible for developing the strategic plan that brings the eight components of health education together into a comprehensive school health program. The strategic plan is developed based on the reports and recommendations of the working groups. The plan should include overall goals to be achieved over the next five years. Target goals should be established for each year, and specific activities and tasks should be identified for the next two years.

The strategic plan serves the following functions:

- Provides a proposal for a comprehensive plan to support the healthy development of children and youth based upon community aspirations and epidemologic data.

- Brings the recommendations of each of the eight working groups into a comprehensive school health program.

- Establishes overall program goals as well as goal statements for each of the eight areas.

- Identifies specific outcome objectives to be accomplished during the first two years of the program.

- Outlines activities to meet each year one objective.

- Establishes a timeline for activities and accomplishment of year one objectives.

- Identifies the staff responsible and the resources, materials and staffing necessary to carry out year one activities.

- Establishes a framework and describes the plans for process, impact and outcome evaluation activities.

The draft of the strategic plan should be shared with all those involved with the planning process for comment and possible revision prior to its official release and subsequent implementation. This will allow individuals involved in each working group to view the work of their group in the context of a comprehensive plan.

STEP 14

Establish Annual Reviews

The Committee for Healthy Students should meet annually to review the status of all past-year activities and to (re)establish the strategic plan for the next year. The committee needs to

- Review progress toward established objectives.

- Review and make decisions on needed modifications and changes related to activities, personnel, resources and materials.

- Review working groups' recommendations for objectives and activities for the upcoming year.

- Establish the next year's objectives and activities and identify resources and materials needed to meet those objectives.

- Develop a report to the school board and community which highlights the achievements of the past year.

Every two years, the Committee for Healthy Students needs to reestablish the five-year plan for the comprehensive school health program. This process should include the following steps:

- Host communitywide meetings to secure new input and identify any changes in the community's aspirations and perceptions of the health needs of children and youth.

- Review the epidemiologic data regarding health status and risky behavior of the community's children and youth.

- Revisit the vision statement to determine necessary modifications.

- Revisit the five-year program goals and make necessary modifications.

Figure 8 provides an outline of an effective review procedure.

STEP 15

Determine Evaluation Procedures for the Program

Evaluating the health program once it is established is important for several reasons. Thoughtfully designed evaluation strategies will provide data about daily activities, management, strategies, learning experiences and community involvement (process evaluation); data about the health knowledge, skills and behaviors of children and youth (impact evaluation); and data about longitudinal changes in health status indicators (outcome evaluation).

Figure 8

Annual Review of Working Groups and the Committee for Healthy Students

Statement of Relationship of Component to Overall Vision:

Working group members should determine if the statement is still valid and expresses the contribution this area can make to the overall efforts to promote the healthy development of children and youth.

Committee for Healthy Students members should determine if the statement of vision is still valid and expresses the school's and community's intent to systematically upgrade programs to promote the healthy development of children and youth.

Review of Five-Year Goals:

Group or committee members should determine if the long-range goals are appropriate in light of school district and community changes. Modification of existing goals, or addition of new goals are usually the actions that are required.

Review of Year-One Objectives and Strategies

Group or committee members should review progress made on each objective during year one. The answers to several questions must be addressed regarding year one objectives:

1. Were the objectives met during year one? If so, is it necessary to take additional action during year two? Is it necessary to maintain the program or activity?

2. If an objective was not met during year one, should the objective and its programs and activities be carried over and continued in year two? Should programs and activities be continued in a modified form? Do new activities, programs and strategies need to be developed for year two?

Figure 8 continued

Identify Objectives for the Upcoming Year:

Objectives for the upcoming year will include those maintenance objectives and unmet objectives carried over from the previous year as well as new objectives targeted for action during the upcoming year. Working groups will recommend these objectives to the Committee for Healthy Students. The committee will base its objectives on the recommendations of the working groups.

Identify Strategies for Meeting Each Objective:

Strategies for meeting objectives may include:
- new policies or procedures
- training or inservice education programs for staff and faculty
- implementation of new programs or utilization of new materials
- school- or community-based activities or events

Identify Resources Needed for Strategies to Meet the Objectives:

Identify any new resources needed to carry out the strategies and accomplish the proposed objectives.

Resources may include:
- new supplies or materials
- new or re-education staff
- new or modified facilities or equipment
- different (healthy) food supplies
- new or modified programs (e.g., peer-led education)

Process Evaluation

Process evaluation activities enable school staff to gather information regarding the quality of services, learning and teaching, program implementation and other activities. Examples of process evaluation include student evaluation of classroom learning activities, teachers' evaluation of the support and management that enables them to deliver effective programs, and evaluation of the food available to students in the school cafeteria.

For students to learn, develop skills and practice healthy behaviors, many things are necessary. Learning materials and activities must be appropriate, teaching and management of the school and program must be effective, opportunities to practice healthy behaviors must be offered, and social norms and individual attention that reinforce students' healthy behavior must be present.

Many of the worksheets provided in Section 2 are designed to enable school leaders to gather process evaluation data. In some cases, evaluation instruments that provide information on the effectiveness of teaching and support and management from school officials will need to be developed.

Process evaluation instruments need not be complicated. The purpose of process evaluation is not to make final decisions regarding the quality of programs. Rather, such evaluation enables school leaders to gather information that can provide infor-mation and answer questions about students', teachers', families' and community members' perceptions of the quality of the program strategies. Information gathered via process evaluation activities can then be used to

- improve services, instruction and support
- modify existing strategies and programs
- reallocate staff and financial resources

Process evaluation should be ongoing, and the data collected should be continually reviewed and used to improve existing programs.

Impact Evaluation

Evaluation activities to measure the impact of the programs also need to be built into the overall plan. Impact evaluation should be conducted on a periodic basis. Examples of impact evaluation include:

- pre- and posttests to measure students' health knowledge and skills
- instruments that measure students' intent to practice healthy behaviors
- measures of health-related behaviors (e.g., prevalence of smoking or cardiovascular related fitness)
- periodic nutrient analysis of the food that students select in the cafeteria

Impact evaluation collects data that measures the program's effectiveness in producing gains in knowledge and achievements in the health behaviors that the program targeted. Impact evaluation will be based on the specific objectives developed in Step 10.

School leaders should conduct an annual review of impact evaluation data. This review should guide planning for upcoming years.

Outcome Evaluation

Outcome evaluation attempts to measure changes in health status over periods of time—usually years. For example, if your program is successful in delaying the onset of or reducing alcohol use among teenagers, you might expect to see:

- a reduction of injuries and deaths resulting from motor vehicle crashes

- a reduction in unintended pregnancies and sexually transmitted disease

- a reduction of injuries and death from violent acts

Improved health status outcomes are the intended goals of health education and health promotion programs. They can only be measured by careful, longitudinal analysis of health status data.

However, school leaders need to understand the importance of small changes in health status indicators. For example, a community that can prevent ten unwanted pregnancies has actually saved hundreds of thousands of dollars and provided ten young women the opportunity to continue with their schooling and develop to their fullest potential.

Preventing one young person from beginning to drink and encountering the subsequent health, social and legal problems many young people experience due to alcohol use may be the difference between that young person becoming productive, paying taxes and contributing to society or being chronically unhappy, sick, unemployed, destructive, in jail and a financial and social burden on the community. School leaders should view the relatively small health status changes detected by outcome evaluations with this perspective.

Process, impact and outcome evaluation strategies need to be built into the health education program plan from the beginning.

STEP 16

Committee for Healthy Students Secures Board of Education Approval and Funding

The school district's board of education has the ultimate responsibility and power to make programmatic and funding decisions to support programs for the healthy development of children and youth. The school board establishes the priorities and identifies the funding necessary to implement a program. It is the Committee for Healthy Student's responsibility to advise the board of education.

Ideally, several board members will be involved in the committees working on development of the program. The Committee for Healthy Students needs to provide ongoing progress reports to the board of education during the developmental stages. These reports and involvement of specific board members will lay the foundation for informed decisions.

A presentation for the board, faculty and staff, and interested community members should be carefully prepared. That presentation should include:

- the community's aspirations for its children and youth (identified in Step 2)

- the needs of the community's children and youth (identified in Step 3)

- the vision for healthy children and youth (identified in Step 6)

- the goals and objectives of the comprehensive school health program (identified in Step 10)

- the proposed plans for meeting the health needs of students (identified in Step 13)

- the request for resources needed to carry out the plan (identified in Step 13)

STEP 17

Staff Implement the Plan

The Committee for Healthy Students and the working groups provide excellent and appropriate opportunities to involve community members in identifying aspirations and developing the vision, goals, objectives and plan. However, committees are not viable mechanisms for implementing plans that establish systematic programs.

Implementation of the school-based activities and programs to support the healthy growth and development of children and youth are the responsibility of teachers and other school personnel. A clear blueprint that identifies each program goal and the objectives and activities related to that goal must be established.

A numbering system that allows for easy reference should be used to identify each activity. Figure 9 shows a sample blueprint. In this example, Goal 3, Objective 1, Activity 1 is written as 3.1.1.

The blueprint includes the following items:

- Goals—The overall goal should be identified first. This broad goal, a general statement of what is to be achieved, could have several specific objectives for year one.

- Specific Objectives—Each goal might have several objectives that need to be met before the achievement of the goal becomes a reality. The example shows one such objective under the broader goal.

- Activities—Activities designed to enable each objective to be met should be clearly identified in the blueprint.

- Individual(s) Responsible—It is important to identify the individual(s) responsible for implementing and supporting each activity. Failure to identify the individual(s) responsible often leads to confusion and delays in the implementation of activities.

- Timeline—Establishing a timeline on which to project completion of activi-

ties increases program success. In order for objectives to be reached, careful and timely coordination of activities is essential. Each activity should be scheduled on the timeline. Figure 10 provides an example of activities scheduled on the year one timeline.

- Materials and Resources—Materials and resources needed for each activity should be identified as early as possible in the planning process. Securing the highest quality materials requires advance planning. Identifying material needs early will contribute to the activities' success.

STEP 18

Staff Monitor Evaluation Data and Report Progress

Continual monitoring of activities and strategies is essential for smooth and successful implementation of the comprehensive school health program. Ongoing process evaluation (Step 15) will provide data that will allow staff to make adjustments in program activities.

Staff meetings at which staff can review the progress with the Committee for Healthy Students should be held monthly. A brief report to the board of education should be

Figure 9
Sample Blueprint

Goal 3: *Involve all students in daily fitness activities which promote healthy physical development*

Objective 3.1: Provide all teachers in grades 1–6 with necessary knowledge and skills to provide daily fitness activities for children and youth.

Activity 3.1.1: Review the literature to determine knowledge and skills needed by teachers to implement appropriate fitness programs for school-age children and youth.

Individual(s) Responsible: Assistant Superintendent will contract with consultant

Materials and Resources Needed:

- Literature reviews of school-based fitness programs
- Evaluation studies of fitness programs
- Expert consultant(s)

Activity 3.1.2: Develop inservice training modules designed to enable all teachers to provide daily fitness activities for children and youth. Develop process and impact evaluation instruments.

Individual(s) Responsible: District Coordinator for Physical Education

Materials and Resources Needed:

- Examples of other training modules
- Example evaluation instruments
- Materials to provide learning experiences (videos, guides, equipment)

Activity 3.1.3: Secure faculty to conduct inservice training of teachers.

Individual(s) Responsible: District Curriculum Coordinator

Materials and Resources Needed:

- Listing of fitness experts in local community, university, state

Figure 9 continued

Activity 3.1.4: Secure facilities and schedule inservice training sessions.

Individual(s) Responsible: Secretary for District Curriculum Coordinator

Materials and Resources Needed:

- Schedule of events and sites planned for the school year
- Listing of possible facilities and contact person and telephone number to reserve those rooms

Activity 3.1.5: Develop and circulate announcements of inservice education for all teachers.

Individual(s) Responsible: District Curriculum Coordinator

Materials and Resources Needed:

- Completed announcement
- Listing of all teachers and addresses

Activity 3.1.6: Conduct first inservice education session for teachers.

Individual(s) Responsible: Consultants

Materials and Resources Needed:

- Equipment: overhead projector; VCR
- Facilities: exercise mats

Activity 3.1.7: Review evaluation data. Modify the inservice based on the evaluation results.

delivered monthly. Special achievements and problems should be identified in these monthly meetings.

Staff should also be responsible for developing, implementing, analyzing data and reporting on the results of impact evaluations. Annual reports on the program's impact on specific objectives should be prepared for the community and the board of education.

Figure 10
Sample Implementation Timeline

Activity	Individual(s) responsible	Sept	Oct	Nov	Dec	Jan	Feb	Mar	April	May	June
3.1.1	Assistant Superintendent/ Consultant	X——————X									
3.1.2	District Coordinator for Physical Education			X—————————X							
3.1.3	District Curriculum Coordinator				X——X						
3.1.4	Secretary for District Curriculum Coordinator					X					
3.1.5	District Curriculum Coordinator						X				
3.1.6	Consultants							X			
3.1.7	Consultants								X——————X		

Outcome evaluation that explores the impact of the program on the health status of children and youth can best be collected and interpreted by public health and social services professionals. School leaders should enter into agreements with these agencies for collection, analysis and interpretation of health status data. An annual report on the health status of children and youth should be prepared for the community and the board of education.

STEP 19

Establish Annual Meetings to Review Progress and Plan the Next Year

Annually, school leaders need to bring together the Committee for Healthy Students, working groups, family and community members, students and school personnel to review the past year's progress and begin the process of planning for the upcoming year. The review of progress provides an excellent opportunity to commend and bask in the successes of the previous year. It also provides the community with a sense of accomplishment that often empowers them to continue with the program. This meeting marks the beginning of a new round of planning for the continuation of the comprehensive school health program.

Planning for and providing school-based programs which facilitate the healthy development of children and youth is a massive undertaking. It requires bringing the entire community together to develop a vision and a commitment to investing in our children and youth. Long-range goals and specific objectives need to be articulated. The boundless energy, time and expertise of many individuals, as well as cooperation among school personnel, families and community members, is required to achieve the goals. Allocation of staffing and other resources are critical to the success of the program. A management plan is essential to ensure a systematic approach. The step-by-step approach given here provides school leaders with a framework for developing school-based comprehensive health programs for children and youth.

Worksheets

Worksheet 1

School Health Education

How established are the following aspects of comprehensive school health education in your school?

	Established Not — Well

A "vision" for school health education that is clearly stated, widely accepted and commonly shared 1 2 3 4 5 6 7

Curriculum advisory committee with representation from health professionals, civic leaders, family members and students 1 2 3 4 5 6 7

Curriculum based on epidemiological diagnosis of the health problems of school-age children 1 2 3 4 5 6 7

Curriculum that reflects the priorities of the local community 1 2 3 4 5 6 7

Curriculum that builds sequentially throughout the grades 1 2 3 4 5 6 7

Curriculum that, overall, addresses all the ten content areas for health education 1 2 3 4 5 6 7

Curriculum that includes a focus on health skills development 1 2 3 4 5 6 7

Curriculum that includes a focus on providing students the opportunities to practice the knowledge and skills learned in the classroom 1 2 3 4 5 6 7

Curriculum that includes learning activities to involve family members and community experiences 1 2 3 4 5 6 7

A process that facilitates a routine annual review of the curriculum.............. 1 2 3 4 5 6 7

Teachers prepared to implement health education 1 2 3 4 5 6 7

Routine health education inservice to strengthen teachers' skills and keep knowledge up to date 1 2 3 4 5 6 7

Adequate budget for health education curricular materials, teaching supplies, inservice education and supervision 1 2 3 4 5 6 7

Two to three hours of health instruction weekly in each elementary grade 1 2 3 4 5 6 7

Sixty to seventy hours of health instruction in each of grades seven and eight 1 2 3 4 5 6 7

Two semesters of health education at the high school level 1 2 3 4 5 6 7

Sufficient material to support the curriculum and teachers in class instruction 1 2 3 4 5 6 7

Formal mechanisms for integrating classroom instruction with the other comprehensive school health program components 1 2 3 4 5 6 7

Ongoing opportunities for community members to be involved in planning and instruction 1 2 3 4 5 6 7

Total School Health Education Score: ____/133

School Environment

How established are your school site's *emergency procedures* for taking quick action to assert control of playgrounds, schoolyards and buildings in the following situations?

Established
Not — Well

Gang member disruptions 1 2 3 4 5 6 7

Drug-related situations (i.e., selling, buying, possession, overdose) 1 2 3 4 5 6 7

Bomb scares, terrorists, weapons on campus 1 2 3 4 5 6 7

Fires, earthquakes, gas leaks, other unexpected mishaps..................1 2 3 4 5 6 7

Death of a student or staff member 1 2 3 4 5 6 7

Suicide of a student, staff member or prominent community member 1 2 3 4 5 6 7

Emergency Procedures Score: ___/42

How adequate is your school district's *emergency communication system* in the following areas?

Adequate
Not — Very

Classroom to classroom 1 2 3 4 5 6 7

Classroom to office...1 2 3 4 5 6 7

Office to buses 1 2 3 4 5 6 7

School to district office 1 2 3 4 5 6 7

School to other schools 1 2 3 4 5 6 7

School to police 1 2 3 4 5 6 7

School to fire department 1 2 3 4 5 6 7

School to electric company 1 2 3 4 5 6 7

School to paramedics 1 2 3 4 5 6 7

School to disaster center...1 2 3 4 5 6 7

Emergency Communications Score: ___/70

Worksheet 2 continued

Does your school have policies and procedures for handling the following situations?

Established
Not — Well

Sale and possession of alcohol and other drugs 1 2 3 4 5 6 7

Possession of weapons (guns, knives, etc.) 1 2 3 4 5 6 7

Universal precautions for handling blood and other body fluids..............................1 2 3 4 5 6 7

Tobacco use by students and staff on campus 1 2 3 4 5 6 7

Physical violence 1 2 3 4 5 6 7

Policy Score: ____/35

How would you rate your school's emphasis on the following *health and safety* areas?

Emphasis
Low — High

Sanitation, lighting, heat control, trash, noise control...1 2 3 4 5 6 7

Cleanliness, attractiveness, landscaping 1 2 3 4 5 6 7

Compliance with and establishment of health and safety policies and procedures 1 2 3 4 5 6 7

Protection of students and teachers from violence, drug pushers,
unwelcome visitors and harassment 1 2 3 4 5 6 7

Health and Safety Score: ____/28

Worksheet 2 continued

What emphasis does your school place on activities to promote positive health?

Emphasis
Low — High

Involving students in promoting a healthy school environment 1 2 3 4 5 6 7

Displaying creative work of students 1 2 3 4 5 6 7

Empowering teachers to be healthy physical, social and emotional role models 1 2 3 4 5 6 7

Establishing high expectations for all students 1 2 3 4 5 6 7

Fostering high self-esteem 1 2 3 4 5 6 7

Promoting social and scholastic success 1 2 3 4 5 6 7

Providing students opportunities to participate and have responsible roles
within the school 1 2 3 4 5 6 7

Providing opportunities for students to practice healthy behaviors 1 2 3 4 5 6 7

Reinforcing healthy behaviors of students and teachers 1 2 3 4 5 6 7

Caring for and supporting students and teachers 1 2 3 4 5 6 7

Health Promotion Score: ____/70

Total Healthy School Environment Score: ____/245

School Health Services

What school health services does your school provide?

Established
Not — Well

Secures a health status profile on each student entering school. 1 2 3 4 5 6 7

Maintains a current up-to-date health record on all enrolled students. 1 2 3 4 5 6 7

Ensures childhood immunization for admittance to school. 1 2 3 4 5 6 7

Provides for routine vision and hearing screening for all students. 1 2 3 4 5 6 7

Provides for mental health evaluations, counseling and referral. 1 2 3 4 5 6 7

Provides for dental health screening and referral. 1 2 3 4 5 6 7

Provides fluoridated dental rinse, toothbrushes, toothpaste and
dental floss for students. 1 2 3 4 5 6 7

Ensures that all students have access to physical and mental health
and dental care. 1 2 3 4 5 6 7

Provides emergency care for injury and sudden illness. 1 2 3 4 5 6 7

Systematically alerts teachers regarding student health issues that
may require special educational considerations. 1 2 3 4 5 6 7

Provides assistance to all teachers in preparing individual educational
programs to meet unique health needs of students. 1 2 3 4 5 6 7

Coordinates management of special health needs of students
during school hours. 1 2 3 4 5 6 7

Provides speech therapy for students. 1 2 3 4 5 6 7

Ensures rapid health and legal response in cases of possible child abuse. 1 2 3 4 5 6 7

Has a system for teachers' referral of suspected health problems. 1 2 3 4 5 6 7

Has a system for diagnosis, referral, treatment and rehabilitation
of student health problems. 1 2 3 4 5 6 7

Provides inservice for teachers and staff to help them identify, refer and
manage students with special health needs. 1 2 3 4 5 6 7

Has a mechanism established for routinely meeting with community
health care providers to discuss health care for children. 1 2 3 4 5 6 7

Encourages abstinence and provides family planning counseling and
services for students. 1 2 3 4 5 6 7

Has a mechanism for securing health care for families of students. 1 2 3 4 5 6 7

All students can secure routine health care services...1 2 3 4 5 6 7

Total School Health Services Score: ___/147

School-Based Physical Education

How established are the following aspects of a physical education program at your school?

	Established *Not — Well*
All students participate in daily physical education.	1 2 3 4 5 6 7
At least 50 percent of the physical education classroom time is spent in physical activity.	1 2 3 4 5 6 7
Teachers have curriculum sequentially developed by grade and developmental level of students.	1 2 3 4 5 6 7
All physical education specialists have teaching certificates in physical education.	1 2 3 4 5 6 7
All classroom teachers responsible for physical education activities of students have had preservice or inservice physical education preparation.	1 2 3 4 5 6 7
The school physical education program works closely with other community-based physical activity programs.	1 2 3 4 5 6 7
The activities of the physical education program are closely integrated with classroom learning in health education.	1 2 3 4 5 6 7
At least 70 percent of the physical education classroom time in upper grades is devoted to lifetime physical activities.	1 2 3 4 5 6 7
The school physical education program includes schoolwide activities that promote involvement and participation.	1 2 3 4 5 6 7
Families and community members are routinely involved in school-based physical education activities.	1 2 3 4 5 6 7
Teachers are trained to adapt physical education programs to meet the special needs of all students.	1 2 3 4 5 6 7
Teachers and staff have opportunities to participate in school-based physical activities.	1 2 3 4 5 6 7

Total School-Based Physical Education Score: ____/84

School Nutrition and Food Services

How established are these nutrition and food services at your school?

Established
Not — Well

Inservice nutrition education is routinely provided for food service personnel. 1 2 3 4 5 6 7

The school food service program closely follows the *Dietary Guidelines for Americans*. 1 2 3 4 5 6 7

Point-of-choice nutritional information is routinely provided in the school food program. 1 2 3 4 5 6 7

Food service personnel work closely with health services personnel to meet special needs of students. 1 2 3 4 5 6 7

Fundraising activities involve only healthy food. 1 2 3 4 5 6 7

Students have the opportunity to choose healthy food for school meals. 1 2 3 4 5 6 7

Onsite vending machines offer healthy food. 1 2 3 4 5 6 7

School has written policies regarding nutritional value of food served at school. 1 2 3 4 5 6 7

Food service personnel routinely work with teachers in classroom instruction. 1 2 3 4 5 6 7

Food service personnel routinely work with teachers to understand how they can further the objectives of classroom instruction. 1 2 3 4 5 6 7

Total School Nutrition and Food Services Score: ____/70

School-Based Counseling and Personal Support

How established are the following counseling services at your school?

Established
Not — Well

Inservice education focusing on students' culture is routinely provided for
school counselors and psychologists. 1 2 3 4 5 6 7

School counselors and psychologists are included on the team that works to
create healthy schools. 1 2 3 4 5 6 7

School counselors work closely with the health instruction component, providing
support in life skills training for students. 1 2 3 4 5 6 7

Counselors work closely with health services personnel to meet special health
needs of students. 1 2 3 4 5 6 7

Counselors and psychologists work closely with families regarding special health
needs of students. 1 2 3 4 5 6 7

Counselors and psychologists work closely with community health and social
services providers. 1 2 3 4 5 6 7

School has formed a partnership with families and community agencies focusing
on the mental/emotional needs of students. 1 2 3 4 5 6 7

Counselors conduct training to help parents and families develop skills that
support the healthy development of their children. 1 2 3 4 5 6 7

Counseling personnel routinely work with teachers in health-related classroom
instruction. 1 2 3 4 5 6 7

Counseling personnel provide leadership on schoolwide mental and emotional
health promotion programs. 1 2 3 4 5 6 7

Counselors and psychologists routinely provide direct services for teachers and
school staff. 1 2 3 4 5 6 7

Counselors and psychologists routinely act as advocates for the mental/emotional
health of students. 1 2 3 4 5 6 7

Crisis teams deal with overdose, injury or death of student(s) or staff. 1 2 3 4 5 6 7

Peer helper programs provide training and support for peer intervention. 1 2 3 4 5 6 7

Student assistance programs identify, screen and refer students and staff with
problems related to alcohol and drug use. 1 2 3 4 5 6 7

Support groups facilitated by trained counselors are provided for students
and staff. 1 2 3 4 5 6 7

Counseling Services Score: _____/112

Worksheet 6 continued

How satisfied are you with the school's counseling services in the following areas?

Satisfied
Not — Very

Divorce and family problems 1 2 3 4 5 6 7

Substance use by students...1 2 3 4 5 6 7

Parents' substance use affecting students...1 2 3 4 5 6 7

Teen sexuality 1 2 3 4 5 6 7

Family planning and pregnancy counseling 1 2 3 4 5 6 7

Depression and suicide 1 2 3 4 5 6 7

Students' problems with friends 1 2 3 4 5 6 7

Sexual and physical abuse..1 2 3 4 5 6 7

Career counseling...1 2 3 4 5 6 7

Academic counseling 1 2 3 4 5 6 7

Youth employment...1 2 3 4 5 6 7

Counseling Satisfaction Score: ____/77

How prepared are your counselors to provide support to students in the following areas?

Prepared
Not — Well

Divorce and family problems	1 2 3 4 5 6 7
Substance use by students	1 2 3 4 5 6 7
Parents' substance use affecting students	1 2 3 4 5 6 7
Teen sexuality	1 2 3 4 5 6 7
Family planning and pregnancy counseling	1 2 3 4 5 6 7
Depression and suicide	1 2 3 4 5 6 7
Students' problems with friends	1 2 3 4 5 6 7
Sexual and physical abuse	1 2 3 4 5 6 7
Career counseling	1 2 3 4 5 6 7
Academic counseling	1 2 3 4 5 6 7
Youth employment	1 2 3 4 5 6 7

Counselors' Preparation Score: ____/77

What best describes your school counseling efforts to support students' development of health-related skills in the following areas?

Developed
Not — Highly

Programs to build self-esteem	1 2 3 4 5 6 7
Programs to help students address loss of control	1 2 3 4 5 6 7
Programs to help students resist peer pressure	1 2 3 4 5 6 7
Programs to help students develop problem-solving skills	1 2 3 4 5 6 7
Programs addressing adolescent issues	1 2 3 4 5 6 7
Programs to help students develop assertiveness skills	1 2 3 4 5 6 7

Counseling Programs Score: ____/42

Total School-Based Counseling and Personal Support Score: ____/308

Schoolsite Health Promotion

What priority does your school give to these health promotion activities?

***Priority
Low — High***

Fully utilizing school facilities to promote health 1 2 3 4 5 6 7

Providing healthy food choices for teachers and staff in the school cafeteria 1 2 3 4 5 6 7

Providing a smoke-free environment 1 2 3 4 5 6 7

Providing an environment free of alcohol and other drugs 1 2 3 4 5 6 7

Sponsoring smoking cessation classes 1 2 3 4 5 6 7

Sponsoring exercise and fitness classes 1 2 3 4 5 6 7

Sponsoring weight control classes 1 2 3 4 5 6 7

Providing routine health screenings (e.g., blood pressure, cholesterol) for staff 1 2 3 4 5 6 7

Providing employee assistance programs for screening, referral, counseling and
rehabilitation for staff 1 2 3 4 5 6 7

Offering self-improvement classes 1 2 3 4 5 6 7

Working with communities to ensure existence of policies and laws that support
healthy behavior 1 2 3 4 5 6 7

Stressing a prevention focus for school health and counseling and
psychological services 1 2 3 4 5 6 7

Sponsoring education that enables school personnel to develop a health-promoting
environment 1 2 3 4 5 6 7

Having teachers who are healthy physical, social and emotional role models 1 2 3 4 5 6 7

Working with families to increase their ability to provide opportunities to practice
and reinforce healthy behaviors 1 2 3 4 5 6 7

Total Schoolsite Health Promotion Score: ____/105

School, Family and Community Health Promotion Efforts

What describes your school's current efforts on the following activities to promote partnerships for healthy development of your students?

Effort
Low — High

The school participates in a health coalition with community members, health and social agencies and parents. 1 2 3 4 5 6 7

The school shares information with collaborating community agencies. 1 2 3 4 5 6 7

Partnerships include representation from a variety of cultures and income levels. 1 2 3 4 5 6 7

The school serves as a center of community activities during non-school hours. 1 2 3 4 5 6 7

Students have an opportunity to engage in community service. 1 2 3 4 5 6 7

Teachers are educated in working in collaboration with community and
family members. 1 2 3 4 5 6 7

Teachers are provided sufficient time to work in collaboration with professionals
and community and family members. 1 2 3 4 5 6 7

Teachers routinely visit the families and homes of students. 1 2 3 4 5 6 7

Teachers routinely assign health-related learning activities that involve students'
families. 1 2 3 4 5 6 7

School and teachers routinely work with health and social service professionals. 1 2 3 4 5 6 7

The school routinely negotiates students' health needs with health care providers. ...1 2 3 4 5 6 7

Health workers are routinely involved in school and classroom teaching and
learning activities...1 2 3 4 5 6 7

Parent education programs on health topics are routinely offered. 1 2 3 4 5 6 7

Family and community members have a voice in the school's health
education programs. 1 2 3 4 5 6 7

The school shares mutual aspirations and visions for students with families and
the community. 1 2 3 4 5 6 7

Money is routinely budgeted for collaboration with community organizations. 1 2 3 4 5 6 7

Clear and mutual goals for the health of students have been agreed on by the
school, families and the community. 1 2 3 4 5 6 7

Group meetings between the school and community are frequent and ongoing. 1 2 3 4 5 6 7

Staff person is assigned the responsibility for creating partnerships focusing on
healthy youth. 1 2 3 4 5 6 7

The school shares a sense of ownership with families and communities regarding
the healthy vision for youth. 1 2 3 4 5 6 7

Total School, Family and Community Health Promotion Score: ____/140

Committee for Healthy Students
Potential Members

Organization	Phone #	Has Health Education Program		Contact Person
		Yes	No	
Community-Based Organizations		☐ ☐	☐ ☐	
Parent Organizations		☐	☐	
Youth Serving Organizations		☐	☐	
Voluntary Health Organizations		☐ ☐	☐	
Social Organizations		☐ ☐	☐ ☐	
Private Businesses/Industry		☐ ☐	☐ ☐	
Health Care Providers		☐	☐	
Health Care Facilities		☐ ☐	☐ ☐	
Community Support Groups		☐ ☐	☐	
Churches		☐ ☐	☐ ☐	
Institutions of Higher Education		☐ ☐	☐ ☐	
Law Enforcement Agencies		☐ ☐	☐	

Priority of Needs for Programs, Services, Policies and Activities

Criterion   *Needs*

1. _____   2. _____   3. _____

number of students
affected   _____   _____   _____

magnitude of the
problem or issue
(on a scale of 1 to 10)   _____   _____   _____

readiness of the
school (1–10)   _____   _____   _____

readiness of the
community (1–10)   _____   _____   _____

potency of
strategy (1–10)   _____   _____   _____

administrative
ease (1–10)   _____   _____   _____

workload required (1–10)   _____   _____   _____

level of community
awareness
necessary (1–10)   _____   _____   _____

level of inservice
training necessary (1–10)   _____   _____   _____

resources available (1–10)   _____   _____   _____

costs of action   _____   _____   _____

costs of inaction   _____   _____   _____

time until completion   _____   _____   _____

Program Goals and Objectives

Program Goal

_____

_____

_____

Program Objectives

1. _____

_____

_____

2. _____

_____

_____

3. _____

_____

_____

4. _____

_____

_____

5. _____

_____

_____

Sample Program Goal and Objectives

Program Goal

To provide healthy lunches and snacks for students

Program Objectives

1. All meals provided by the school cafeteria to students and staff will contain less than 25 percent of calories from fats.

2. All schools will serve only juices and water (no soda pop) in drink vending machines.

Sample Comprehensive Health Programs Self-Assessment*

Santa Cruz County Office of Education
Health Education Advisory Committee

The following self-assessment instrument was developed by the Santa Cruz County Office of Education Health Education Advisory Committee. It is an excellent example of the type of assessment tool local school districts will want to use to evaluate current efforts as they develop a comprehensive school health program.

*Reprinted with permission from the Santa Cruz County Office of Education, Educational Services Division.

A. Health Education

1.   Does your present curriculum address the following areas?
     a. healthy life style promotion
     b. disease prevention
     c. risk factor reduction
     d. self-esteem development
     e. decision-making skills

2.   Does your present curriculum address the following topics?
     a. nutrition
     b. mental and emotional well-being
     c. physical growth and development
     d. consumer health

3.   Does your present curriculum address the following topics?
     a. family life education
     b. substance use and abuse
     c. disease and disorders
     d. health related physical fitness

4.   Does your district have a planned sequential health education curriculum for Grades K–3?
     a. yes
     b. in process
     c. no

5.   Does your district have a planned sequential health education curriculum for Grades 4 and 5?
     a. yes
     b. in process
     c. no

6.   Does your district have a planned sequential health education curriculums for Grades 6–8?
     a. yes
     b. in process
     c. no

7. Does your district have a planned sequential health education curriculum for Grades 9–12?
    a. yes
    b. in process
    c. no

8. Are health topics taught along with the following subject areas?
    a. science
    b. social science
    c. physical education
    d. home economics
    e. other

9. What resources do you use to support your health education curriculum?
    a. packaged kits
    b. other published materials
    c. voluntary health agency materials
    d. textbooks
    e. district written guides

10. Who provides *district* level leadership in developing/implementing your health education curriculum?
    a. curriculum coordinator
    b. district nurse
    c. teacher
    d. school administrator
    e. health education coordinator

11. Who typically provides leadership and expertise at the individual *elementary* school site for health education?
    a. administrator
    b. school nurse
    c. teacher with special interest in the field
    d. P.E. teacher
    e. other

12. Who typically provides leadership and expertise at the individual *secondary* school site for health education?
    a. certified health education specialist
    b. school nurse
    c. science teacher
    d. home economics teacher
    e. P.E. teacher

13. What are your approaches for carrying out staff development in health education?
    a. district inservice education
    b. schoolsite inservice education
    c. conferences and workshops outside the district
    d. university or other professional growth opportunities for individuals

B. Physical Education

14. Does your district have an articulated P.E. curriculum for all grade levels?
    a. yes
    b. partial
    c. in process—being revised or developed
    d. no

15. Does your *elementary* P.E. curriculum provide experiences in the following areas?
    a. basic movement skills, rhythm and dance
    b. physical fitness
    c. games and sports
    d. others

16. Does your *secondary* P.E. curriculum provide experiences in the following areas?
    a. basic movement skills, rhythm and dance
    b. physical fitness
    c. games, sports and gymnastics
    d. aquatics
    e. combatives

17. What types of sports and activities are offered that can be pursued and enjoyed throughout the students' lives?
    a. tennis/racquetball
    b. golf
    c. swimming
    d. aerobic exercise
    e. running/walking

18. Do P.E. activities provide regular exercise of sufficient intensity and duration to enhance cardiopulmonary efficiency (at least 20 minutes 3 times per week)?
    a. yes
    b. to some extent
    c. no

19. Who provides leadership and expertise at the *district* level for developing/implementing your P.E. curriculum?
    a. curriculum coordinator
    b. P.E. specialist
    c. P.E. teacher or coach from school level
    d. other

20. Who typically provides leadership and expertise at the *elementary* sites for P.E.?
    a. administrator
    b. teacher with special interest in the field
    c. P.E. teacher
    d. other

21. Who typically provides leadership and expertise at the *secondary* sites for P.E.?
    a. P.E. department head
    b. P.E. teacher with special interest in improving instruction
    c. other

C. Health Services

22. How much time is a credentialed school nurse at an elementary school site?
    a. not at all
    b. less than 1 full day a week
    c. 1 day a week
    d. 2–3 days a week
    e. 4–5 days a week

23. How much time is a credentialed school nurse at a middle school site?
    a. not at all
    b. less than 1 full day a week
    c. 1 day a week
    d. 2–3 days a week
    e. 4–5 days a week

24. How much time is a credentialed school nurse at a high school site?
    a. not at all
    b. less than 1 full day a week
    c. 1 day a week
    d. 2–3 days a week
    e. 4–5 days a week

25. Does your district offer any non-mandated direct health services to protect student health and to stop problems that could interfere with learning?
    a. health risk assessment, such as growth and developmental norms, height, weight, body fat, blood pressure and cholesterol
    b. assessment of performance on the California Physical and Health Related Fitness Test.
    c. neurological assessment
    d. only mandated services are available (screening for vision, hearing, scoliosis problems)
    e. other

26. Who reviews health charts to compile information about identified health conditions in order to alert teachers and other staff members to potential problems?
    a. credentialed school nurse
    b. health clerk
    c. school secretary
    d. administrator
    e. other

27. What community health resources does your district use to assist in providing health services?
    a. county health department
    b. voluntary health agencies (e.g., American Cancer Society, American Heart Association, American Lung Association, March of Dimes, etc.)
    c. community health clinics (e.g., Planned Parenthood, etc.)
    d. community service organizations (e.g., Lions Club, etc.)
    e. private physicians and dentists

28. Do you have a school based health clinic staffed by a pediatric nurse practitioner under the direction of a medical doctor?
    a. yes
    b. in the planning stage
    c. in the consideration stage
    d. no

29. Does your district have clearly defined written procedures for providing emergency care?
    a. yes
    b. being developed
    c. not currently available

D. Nutrition Services

30. Does your school district participate in the federally sponsored national meal programs?
    a. breakfast
    b. lunch
    c. both of the above
    d. none of the above

31. How is food service provided at your school sites?
    a. school/district operated cafeterias or central kitchen
    b. food service from outside caterer
    c. snack bar, privately operated
    d. snack bar, operated by school
    e. vending machines

32. If district does not operate its own food service, does the district have any control over the nutritional quality of the food offered?
    a. yes
    b. to some extent
    c. no
    d. N/A

33. On average, what percent of elementary students use food services offered at school?
    a. 25% or less
    b. 26% to 50%
    c. 51% to 75%
    d. Over 75%

34. On average, what percent of middle/junior high students use food services offered at school?
    a. 25% or less
    b. 26% to 50%
    c. 51% to 75%
    d. Over 75%

35. On average, what percent of high school students use food services offered at school?
    a. 25% or less
    b. 26% to 50%
    c. 51% to 75%
    d. Over 75%

36. Does your food service program relate to the nutrition education presented in the classroom?
    a. Foods low in nutrient value (e.g., chips, sodas and candy) are not available.
    b. A certified nutritionist/dietitian plans or approves menus.
    c. Students participate in menu planning.
    d. Menus are available in classrooms.
    e. Parents are informed of food choices available.

37. Who provides leadership and expertise at the district level for your nutrition services program?
    a. certified nutritionist/dietitian
    b. classified employee
    c. consultant
    d. administrator
    e. other

E. Counseling and Psychological Services

38. What grade levels in your district receive counseling/guidance services on a *regularly scheduled* basis?
    a. elementary
    b. middle/junior high
    c. high school
    d. none

39. To which student population groups is your district able to provide counseling/guidance services?
    a. special education students
    b. high risk students
    c. general student population
    d. other

40. In what ways do your guidance and counseling staff work in partnership with teachers?
    a. identifying students at risk
    b. developing plans for students at risk
    c. working directly with parents
    d. making community referrals
    e. other

41. In what ways has your staff been prepared to recognize the warning signs of emotional stress and take the appropriate action?
    a. inservice education within the last two years
    b. annual staff orientation to current policies and procedures related to crisis intervention
    c. new staff orientation to current policies and procedures related to crisis intervention
    d. other

42. In what ways have your staff and parents been prepared to assist in the nurturing of self-esteem for themselves and students?
    a. teacher and administrative staff inservice
    b. classified personnel inservice
    c. parent education
    d. other

43. What do your guidance/counseling staff do to promote a healthy school climate?
    a. provide parent information (e.g., newsletter)
    b. initiate formal and informal contacts with staff to promote an awareness of student needs and counseling services and to develop working partnerships
    c. provide a mechanism for immediate referral and follow-up
    d. provide inservice training to staff
    e. other

44. Who provides leadership and expertise at the district level for developing/implementing your counseling and guidance program?
    a. district administrator
    b. psychologist
    c. private counseling service under contract with district
    d. guidance and counseling specialist
    e. other

F. Safe and Healthy School Environment

45. Do your school sites have procedures for taking quick steps to assert control of playgrounds, schoolyards and hallways in the following situations?
    a. gang member disruptions
    b. drug pushers
    c. bomb scares, terrorist activities, weapons on campus
    d. unauthorized persons on campus
    e. earthquakes, other natural disasters and hazards, such as presence of gas leaks, hazardous materials, accidents, etc.

46. In what situations do you feel that communication in emergency situations in your district is adequate?
    a. classroom to classroom
    b. classroom to office
    c. office to buses
    d. school to district office
    e. school to school

47. Are school sites in your district able to immediately contact the following key agencies?
    a. police/sheriff's departments
    b. fire department
    c. power company
    d. county disaster center
    e. hospital/medical facility

48. In what ways is initiative taken at the school site to improve the school environment?
    a. organizing campus cleanup
    b. recycling of materials
    c. improving landscaping
    d. displaying student art and other creative work
    e. involving students in promoting school environment improvement

49. Who provides district leadership in developing/implementing/maintaining safe and healthy school environments?
    a. district maintenance, transportation and operations supervisor
    b. district administrator
    c. district safety committee
    d. other

G. Health Promotion for Staff

50. In what areas does your district provide health and wellness programs and activities for certificated staff?
    a. exercise programs
    b. nutrition information
    c. stress-management inservices
    d. medical tests and health and fitness appraisals
    e. classes for weight management, smoking cessation, etc.

51. In what areas does your district provide health and wellness programs and activities for classified staff?
    a. exercise programs
    b. nutrition information
    c. stress-management inservices
    d. medical tests, health and fitness appraisals and referral services

52. Who provides district level leadership in developing and implementing health promotion activities?
    a. personnel director
    b. credentialed school nurse
    c. district administrator
    d. teacher
    e. other

53. How are district/school staff assisted with psychological problems or addictive behaviors?
    a. Counseling services are available.
    b. Smoking cessation classes are available.
    c. Support groups are available for chemical substance abuse.
    d. District provides insurance coverage or other assistance for treatment and rehabilitation.
    e. District policies/regulations support health promotion for staff.

H. Parent and Community Involvement

54. Do your district's schools give parents a voice in health program planning by means of community advisory groups?
    a. yes
    b. to some extent
    c. no

55. How are health related volunteers from the community used at the school?
    a. sharing expertise in guest lectures
    b. leading small group discussions
    c. building needed equipment
    d. helping out as needed

56. Are funds from the community solicited for school health programs, e.g., The Metropolitan Life Foundation, Healthy Me Program, etc.?
    a. yes
    b. to some extent
    c. no

57. Parent education programs on topics related to physical, mental/emotional and social health are offered through our schools:
    a. on an annual planned basis
    b. on a crisis as-needed basis
    c. seldom or never
    d. other

58. Who provides district level leadership in recruiting parent and community involvement in school health programs?
    a. district health coordinator
    b. credentialed school nurse
    c. district administrator
    d. counseling/guidance coordinator
    e. community/school advisory committee

Sample Scope and Sequence for a Comprehensive Health Program

The following scope and sequence was developed by ETR Associates for the *Actions for Health* program for grades K through 6. Content indicators provide an overview of the emphasis of content at different levels for a specific program. This scope and sequence is an example of the type of chart that can be used as a planning tool for comprehensive health instruction. School districts will need to create a scope and sequence that meets local needs and interests of learners. This chart serves as an example of an instructional planning and implementation tool.

	Growth and Development	Mental and Emotional Health	Family Life and Health	Nutrition	Substance Use Prevention
K	• teeth	• self-esteem: being unique and different • feelings about being at school • talking about feelings	• family portraits	• foods that help the body • food groups • healthy breakfast foods	• what are poisons • healthy habits • healthy decisions
1	• body parts	• favorite activities • personal uniqueness • special characteristics of peers • identifying feelings • ways to manage feelings	• body parts • variety of families • ways family members care for each other • family activites and traditions	• healthy snacks	• helpful and harmful substances • healthy choices about drugs • importance of not smoking • healthy and unhealthy habits
2	• body parts • characteristics of infants • differences between infants' and toddlers' behavior	• listening skills • communication • body language • positive and negative messages • expressing anger and strong feelings • ways to communicate friendship • coping with stress • communicating appreciation at school	• body parts • family changes • different points of view • communicating appreciation at home	• nutrient-rich foods	• healthy drinks for children • saying no • free-time activities
3		• individual uniqueness • decision making • cooperative and considerate behaviors • characteristics of friendship	• family roles and responsibilities • cooperative and considerate behaviors	• foods that help the body stay healthy • healthy meals and snacks	• techniques for saying no • positive and negative peer pressure • prescription and OTC drugs • reasons not to use alcohol or tobacco • saying no to drugs
4	• body systems • growth and life cycles	• ways to enhance self-esteem • decisions about health and safety • influences on decisions • qualities of friends • positive and negative peer pressure • techniques for saying no	• family values • conflict resolution/negotiation	• nutrients • how the body uses food • five food groups • reading food labels	• safe choices about medicine • reasons for not using drugs or tobacco
5	• growth patterns and puberty	• positive and negative stress • dealing with stress • communication skills • relaxation techniques	• family happiness • sexuality • choosing abstinence • coping with family stresses	• nutrition	• effects and problems of drug use • marijuana and inhalants • influences on drug use decisions • avoiding drug use
6	• prenatal growth and development	• goal-setting process • steps to achieve goals • personal and social skills • ways to say no • coping with stress	• human reproductive process • sexual responsibility — avoiding teen pregnancy • prenatal growth and development • parenting	• nutrition • body image and eating disorders	• ways to say no • steroids • alcohol and alcoholism • healthy alternatives to drug use • avoiding use of needles • peer, school and community resources for drug use prevention

Personal Health and Hygiene	Disease Prevention and Control	Injury Prevention and Safety	Consumer Health	Community and Environmental Health
• hand washing • sunscreen • teeth • five senses	• hand washing	• safety getting to and from school • getting adult help • avoiding injury from weapons		• manners
• dental health • five senses • healthy and unhealthy habits	• how germs are spread • communicable and noncommunicable health problems including HIV/AIDS	• bus safety • pedestrian safety • good and bad touches • preventing accidental poisoning • obtaining help in emergencies	• health helpers	• actions that are good for the environment
• activities that promote fitness • medical check-ups • actions to take when not feeling well	• communicable disease • HIV/AIDS transmission	• simple first-aid • reporting an emergency • fire safety • conflict resolution	• misleading advertising messages • health workers in the community	• health workers in the community
• ways to improve fitness • physical activity • rest and exercise	• avoiding illness, including HIV/AIDS • safe choices about medicine	• making safe decisions • kitchen safety • safety hazards at home and school • safe behaviors in the car • bicycle safety		• air, water and land pollution • the three R's — reduce, reuse, recycle • environmental impact of actions
• benefits of exercise • healthy choices about rest and sleep	• cleanliness and disease prevention • viruses • HIV transmission	• techniques for saying no • positive and negative peer pressure • negotiation • conflict resolution • fire safety	• common advertising techniques • evaluating ads for health care products • reading food labels	• effects of air, water and land pollution • ways to improve the environment
• benefits of exercise • lifestyle choices • hygiene	• chronic-degenerative disease • HIV symptoms, spread and prevention	• preventing recreational injuries • water safety • preventing gun-related injury • rescue breathing and Heimlich maneuver • recognizing and reporting child and sexual abuse	• health quackery • misleading ads for tobacco and alcohol	• health care professionals
• healthy benefits of good grooming	• sexual responsibility • STDs, including HIV/AIDS • public response to disease, including HIV • body image and eating disorders	• ways to say no • drunk driving • risk factors for injury • basic first-aid • suicide prevention	• community health information and services	• personal responsibility for health and environment • volunteer opportunities in health and environment • public response to disease, including HIV

Resources for Comprehensive Health Education

The following organizations provide resources and materials regarding comprehensive health education:

American Alliance for Health, Physical Education, Recreation and Dance, 1900 Association Drive, Reston, VA 22091, (703) 476-3400

AAHPERD membership is made up of professionals in health, physical education, recreation, dance and sports education. It publishes *Physical Best,* a national physical fitness education and assessment program, and coordinates *Jump Rope for Heart,* a special event that educates students about cardiovascular fitness and benefits the American Heart Association.

American Academy of Pediatrics, P.O. Box 927, Elk Grove Village, IL 60007, (800) 433-9016

AAP pursues legislative, community-based, and public-awareness efforts regarding improvement of health for children. It publishes a catalog of publications and services for pediatric health care professionals, including *School Health: A Guide for Health Professionals.*

American Health Foundation, 320 East 43rd Street, New York, NY 10007, (212) 953-1900

AHF develops health education materials, including the *Know Your Body* curriculum for grades K–7.

American Medical Association, 535 North Dearborn Street, Chicago, IL 60610, (312) 645-5315

AMA maintains a Department of Adolescent Health that produces the *AMA Profiles of Adolescent Health,* a series of publications on topics such as the health indicators of American teens, risk-taking behaviors, etc.

American Public Health Association, 1015 15th Street, NW, Washington, DC 20005, (202) 789-5600

APHA represents public health professionals from many occupational roles. A School

Health Special Interest Group is sponsored by APHA and publishes a biannual newsletter for members.

American School Food Service Association, 3620 Galapago Street, Englewood, CO 80110, (800) 525-8575

ASFSA is a not-for-profit, professional organization whose membership includes state and local food service directors and supervisors, cafeteria managers, food service assistants and nutrition educators. ASFSA sponsors National School Lunch Week and publishes *The Healthy Edge in Schools*, a booklet that outlines strategies for implementing healthy food service programs in schools using a "team" approach.

American School Health Association, P.O. Box 708, Kent, OH 44240, (216) 678-1601

ASHA is a membership organization which promotes comprehensive school health. They publish the *Journal of School Health*, as well as a catalog of various health education materials.

Association for the Advancement of Health Education, 1900 Association Drive, Reston, VA 22091, (703) 476-3440

AAHE strives to improve the human condition by supporting education and dynamic health education programs in schools (K-12), colleges and universities, and other settings. It is one of the associations that make up the American Alliance for Health, Physical Education, Recreation and Dance.

Coalition of National Health Education Organizations, c/o Dr. Peter Cortese, 3472 Greystone Circle, Atlanta, GE 30341, (404) 488-5365.

The Coalition of National Health Education Organizations is made up of professional organizations that have identifiable memberships of health educators who have a major commitment to health education within and outside of schools. These organizations include the American College Health Association; American Public Health Association; American School Health Association; Association for the Advancement of Health Education; Conference of State and Territorial Directors of Public Health Education; and the Society of State Directors of Health, Physical Education and Recreation. The Coalition can help schools by serving as a communication and advisory resource on health education issues.

Comprehensive Health Education Foundation, 22323 Pacific Highway South, Seattle, WA 98198, (206) 824-2907, or (800) 323-CHEF

CHEF distributes *Here's Looking at You 2000*, a drug-abuse prevention program for grades K–12. It has also developed a peer education program, other health education programs and materials.

Education Development Center, 55 Chapel Street, Newton, MA 02160, (617) 969-7100

EDC manages the development and dissemination of the *Teenage Health Teaching Modules* (THTM) for junior and senior high school. It also coordinates the Comprehensive School Health Training Network, which provides regional training.

ETR Associates, P.O. Box 1830, Santa Cruz, CA 95061-1830, (800) 321-4407

ETR Associates is a private, nonprofit health education organization that offers a variety of publications for health education, as well as training and research services. It publishes the *Contemporary Health Series* (CHS), which includes *Actions for Health* for grades K–6, *Into Adolescence* for middle school and *Entering Adulthood* for high school.

National Association of School Nurses, P.O. Box 1300, Scarborough, ME 04074, (207) 883-2117

NASN promotes the delivery of quality health programs to the school community by strengthening the professional growth of school nurses and advancing the practice of school nursing. It provides professional training opportunities and cosponsors the certification examination for school nurses.

National Center for Health Education, 30 East 29th Street, New York, NY 10016, (212) 689-1886

The National Center for Health Education manages *Growing Healthy*, a comprehensive health education curriculum for students in grades K–7. Management activities include development of new units, training and evaluation.

National School Boards Association, 1680 Duke Street, Alexandria, VA 22314, (703) 838-6756

NSBA has established a national consortium of organizations committed to student health. Consortium activities are geared toward encouraging school boards across the nation to establish comprehensive health education programs. NSBA also published *School Health: Helping Children Learn* (1991), a guidebook to help school leaders implement comprehensive school health programs.

National School Health Education Coalition, P.O. Box 515664, Dallas, TX 75251-5664, (214) 233-9305

NaSHEC provides a common ground for organizations to work together to meet the goal of providing a comprehensive school health education experience to every student in preschool through grade 12. Membership is primarily made up of national organizations although individuals may subscribe to NaSHEC's newsletter. Through its Legislative Action Group, Inc., NaSHEC supports coalition building at state and local levels to educate and assist decision makers in school health issues. NaSHEC maintains a database and serves as a central source of information about private and public sector organizations with an interest in comprehensive school health education.

References

Allensworth, D. D., and L. J. Kolbe. 1987. The comprehensive school health program: Exploring an expanded concept. *Journal of School Health* 57 (10): 409-412.

American School Health Association, Association for the Advancement of Health Education and Society for Public Health Education. 1989. *National adolescent student health survey*. Oakland, CA: Third Party Press.

Amidei, N. 1990. Crossing the boundaries between health and education. National Health/Education Consortium. Symposium conducted in Washington, D.C.

Benard, B. 1991. Fostering resiliency in kids: Protective factors in the family, school and community. *Western Regional Center for Drug-Free Schools and Communities*. Portland, OR: NWREL.

Berdiansky, H. A., T. T. McKinney and M. W. Richardson. 1992. *Peers empowering peers the action challenge: A resource guide for school/community peer helper teams*. Raleigh, NC: North Carolina State University.

Carnegie Council on Adolescent Development, Task Force on Education of Young Adolescents. 1989. *Turning points: Preparing American youth for the 21st century*. Washington, DC.

Hayes, C. D., ed. 1987. *Risking the future: Adolescent sexuality, pregnancy, and childbearing*. Washington, DC: National Academy Press.

Klingman, A. 1984. Health-related school guidance: Practical application in primary prevention. *Personnel and Guidance Journal* 62: 576-579.

McGinnis, J. M., and C. DeGraw. 1991. Healthy Schools 2000: Creating partnerships for the decade. *Journal of School Health* 61(7): 292-296.

Middleton, K., B. M. Hubbard, W. M. Kane and J. Taylor. 1991. *Making health education comprehensive*. Contemporary Health Series. Santa Cruz, CA: ETR Associates.

National Commission on the Role of the School and Community in Improving Adolescent Health. 1990. *Code blue: Uniting for healthier youth*. Alexandria, VA: National Association of State Boards of Education.

New Mexico Department of Health, Public Health Division. 1989. *New Mexico selected health statistics: Annual report.* Santa Fe, NM.

Noddings, N. 1988. Schools face crisis in caring. *Education Week,* Dec. 7, 1988.

Office of Disease Prevention and Health Promotion. 1984. *Key findings: National children and youth fitness study II.* Washington, DC.

Report of the 1990 Joint Committee on Health Education Terminology. 1991. *Journal of Health Education* 22 (2): 97–108.

Tobler, N. 1986. Meta-analysis of 143 adolescent drug prevention programs: Quantative outcome results of program participants compared to control or comparison group. *Journal of Drug Issues* 16:537-567.

U.S. Congress. Office of Technology Assessment. 1991. *Adolescent health: Summary and policy options.* Washington, DC.

U.S. Department of Health and Human Services. 1988. *National Center for Health Statistics: Annual report.* Washington, DC.

U.S. Department of Health and Human Services, Public Health Service. 1990. Youth risk behavior surveillance system. *Chronic Disease and Health Promotion MMWR Reprints.* Atlanta, GA: Centers for Disease Control and Prevention.

U.S. Department of Health and Human Services, Public Health Service. 1990. *Healthy people 2000: National health promotion and disease prevention objectives.* DHHS Publication No. (PHS) 91-50212. Washington, DC.

Be a Leader in Comprehensive School Health with Other Ground-Breaking Guides from ETR Associates!

(#562-H1)
136 pages
paper

(#580-H1)
160 pages
paper

(#598-H1)
120 pages
paper

(#356-H1)
526 pages
paper

These are just a few of the more than 600 health education resources available from ETR Associates for today's busy administrators and teachers. Call today for more information on innovative books, curricula, pamphlets and videos!

Call 1 (800) 321-4407

or contact:
Sales Department
ETR Associates, P.O. Box 1830, Santa Cruz, CA 95061-1830

FAX: (408) 438-4284